MAKE IT FANCY

MAKE IT FANCY

COOKING AT HOME WITH SAD PAPI

BRANDON SKIER

Photography by Dylan James Ho and Jeni Afuso

Simon Element

New York   London   Toronto   Sydney   New Delhi

SIMON
ELEMENT

An Imprint of Simon & Schuster, Inc.
1230 Avenue of the Americas
New York, NY 10020

First Simon Element hardcover edition March 2024

SIMON ELEMENT is a trademark of Simon & Schuster, Inc.

Simon & Schuster: Celebrating 100 Years of Publishing in 2024

For information about special discounts for bulk purchases, please contact Simon & Schuster Special Sales at 1-866-506-1949 or business@simonandschuster.com.

The Simon & Schuster Speakers Bureau can bring authors to your live event. For more information or to book an event, contact the Simon & Schuster Speakers Bureau at 1-866-248-3049 or visit our website at www.simonspeakers.com.

Food Styling by Brandon Skier

Prop Styling by Jeni Afuso

Manufactured in China

1 3 5 7 9 10 8 6 4 2

Library of Congress Cataloging-in-Publication Data has been applied for.

ISBN 978-1-6680-0424-1

ISBN 978-1-6680-0425-8 (ebook)

CONTENTS

VINAIGRETTES AND DRESSINGS 69

STOCKS AND SAUCES 77

STARTERS..93

LETTUCE AND THINGS..129

PASTAS...153

ACKNOWLEDGMENTS

Barbara Skier, aka Mom: I mean, let's be honest—none of this would have been possible without you. You busted your hump and raised a family as a single mom, and did a damn great job. You even inadvertently set me on course to pursue a career in food. You came to eat at every restaurant I worked in, from the first diners to the Michelin-starred places. Now you watch my videos and call me about the recipes so you can make them with friends. You've always been my number one fan, and I'm so fortunate to have been raised by you.

Neal Fraser and Jason Bowlin: My chefs at Redbird. Besides being great teachers and mentors, you've always encouraged creativity and set me on the path to find my own voice in food.

Remy Park: From beginning to end of the book-writing process, you were always encouraging and my biggest cheerleader.

Anna Worrall: The most kick-ass literary agent I could ask for. You made everything so smooth and easy.

Lauren Miyashiro: We went through this process of my first cookbook, and your first time co-writing a cookbook, together. It was an absolute pleasure, and thank you for making me sound cool and literate.

Dylan James Ho and Jeni Afuso: Thank you for making the photography and styling process so fun and enjoyable. And for making the food look so good.

Rebecca Batchelor: The design is so perfect.

Justin Schwartz and everyone at Simon Element: Thank you for giving me the opportunity to write my first book. Seeing these recipes on paper, I feel so incredibly fortunate.

And last but not least, to my papitas: I love making things fancy with you all.

MY STORY

My desire to cook professionally started early in life. When I was growing up, the men in my family were the ones who did the cooking. My grandpa was a baker in the army, and my dad was a line cook before he went to college, so for the most part, whenever there was food around, they were the ones in the kitchen. They loved pulling me in and having me help, and I loved helping. At the time, shows like *Iron Chef* and *Good Eats* were also very popular, and I was only around ten years old when I told my parents I wanted to go to culinary school. They were really supportive.

But everything took a turn in my preteen years when my dad, grandpa, and grandma were all diagnosed with cancer and eventually passed away within years of each other. My mom started working extra jobs to take care of me and my sister. She didn't have the time to do the cooking, so I took over.

That's when I figured out that food isn't just sustenance. Cooking for someone can communicate that you care, can comfort, and can celebrate.

After a few years of cooking for my household, I got a work permit at age sixteen. I wanted to be a little more self-sufficient to help my mom, so I took the work that was offered to me. My first job was working on cars. I started as a detailer and worked my way up to a parts manager—it was a pretty cushy little job for being so young. The only problem was I hated it. I was sitting at a desk all day, putting on a customer service voice, and generally losing my mind. I didn't get to create anything or work with my hands—and I was always thinking about food.

Finally, I decided to try and find work where my mind kept wandering. I found Jonathan Gold's list of 101 Best Restaurants, which for a while was like the unofficial *Michelin Guide* for Los Angeles, back when the guide didn't include my hometown. I applied to every restaurant that looked interesting and was turned away most of the time because I had no experience. I eventually got a minimum-wage fry-cook job at a trendy fusion and comfort-food place. Then I got a second job doing bread and pastry in the morning somewhere else. I loved it. And the rest is a blur: dinner service here, morning job there, helping with a pop-up this day, catering the next. It stayed like that for years. Every time I wanted to work somewhere new, I pulled up Jonathan Gold's list and started applying. I eventually did go to culinary school, after a few years of working in the industry. But honestly, I think I learned more on the job.

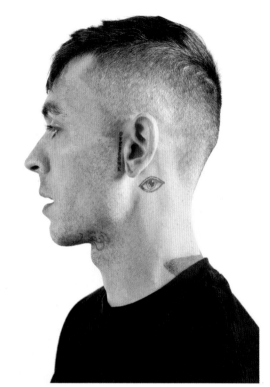

After some time, I landed at Redbird, a restaurant founded by Neal Fraser and his wife, Amy. I loved that place. It was like a living, breathing thing. The dining room could do over 300 covers; there were five private dining rooms, a huge cathedral turned event hall, and an outside garden for additional parties. Working in a place like that makes you really good at time management. The food at Redbird was more elevated, and I worked the line for the dining room, but if any other parties needed help, it was all hands on deck. There was never a dull moment at the Bird. It was wild, and I had a lot of fun.

On my days off, I was staging at other restaurants because I wanted to learn different approaches to food. My friend was a sous chef at a two *Michelin*-star restaurant, and I started going in whenever I could. Eventually, he offered me a job. After starting at the bottom of Jonathan Gold's list, I had finally arrived at the top. It was such an "I did it!" moment.

But then I heard there was a new concept restaurant opening called Auburn. There was so much buzz around it, and the food they were creating was incredible. It was a tasting menu, but the twist was you could order *whatever* you wanted. Six courses of the duck? Cool. Four courses of desserts? Also cool. Want to be bold and go the whole 12-course route? Amazing. Between the food and the concept, I knew I had to work there. And I loved it. You know when you have a job and it's just a job? Yeah, this was different. Auburn felt like home.

Then Covid happened.

Indoor dining was shut down and a lot of restaurants couldn't stay open, including Auburn. I lost my job, and every restaurant I applied to either wasn't hiring or was closing. Out of the desire to keep busy where I was, I started posting short recipe videos on TikTok. It all happened pretty quickly—a few thousand views at first. Then 20,000 views. A million views. Ten million views. Larger creators who were established on other platforms reached out to me and encouraged me to go full time. And after a few weeks thinking about it, I decided to go all in.

I was initially filming on an iPhone 4 with a cracked screen, so first I went out and bought an actual camera. I had never owned a computer before, so I also went to get a laptop. Then, with the help of YouTube, I taught myself how to use editing software. Three years later, I'm still sharing food content across multiple platforms. And I've been featured in the *LA Times*, the *New York Times*, *Eater*, *Fast Company*, and others, and on the BBC. It's what we call "turning a frown upside down." Making the videos has shown me how many people are excited to get fancy at home— and I have inspired millions to try.

HOW TO USE THIS BOOK

A lot of the recipes I share online are items you might order on a menu at some highbrow restaurant, but they're formatted visually here so you can follow along and make them at home. And that's kind of how this book is laid out. Imagine an elevated meal at your house and the components you'd need to put that meal together. I walk you through it.

The Pantry chapter is full of small things I just really enjoy having around, and I encourage you to get creative with how you use them. The rest of the recipes in the book are organized like a menu—there are starters, main courses, desserts, and drinks. The idea is that you pick what you like and put together your meal.

I'll warn you: I made it all fancy. But I also made it doable, and I don't ask you to bust out a combi oven. There are a couple recipes in here that might sound time-consuming or daunting, but they're also meant for something special, not to be made every day.

The most important thing is to just have fun with it.

SPECIAL EQUIPMENT USED IN THIS BOOK

Bench scraper: It's effective for working and shaping doughs. But I also use it all the time while I'm prepping—chop, scoop, and go.

Blender: For making smooth sauces, purees, vinaigrettes, and soups. A high-powered blender, such as a Vitamix, will yield the best results.

Chinois or extra-fine-mesh strainer: For removing all lumps and little bits for a super-smooth texture.

Dehydrator: To slowly dry ingredients to preserve them and to concentrate the flavors, plus so much more. When possible, I give an oven alternative.

Deli slicer: Something fancy I do not expect you to have! But if you do, turn to page 96 right now for an unexpected way to use it.

Digital scale: Some recipes require more precision. But it's also true that weighing ingredients with a scale can be faster and easier than using measuring cups and spoons.

Electric pressure cooker: Things that usually take forever to cook are ready in a fraction of the time. In the case of this book, it's a starting point, used to cook beef tendon before it's sliced thin, dehydrated, and fried into a delicious puff (see page 96).

Fermentation lids: These have small valves that allow gas to escape without your opening the jar. If you don't have one, and don't want to get one, you can instead "burp" the jar by opening the lid every few days.

Fermentation weights: To keep whatever you're fermenting fully submerged.

Food processor: To speed along the fine chopping, though it's optional in most cases.

Instant-read thermometer: It's not just for making sure meat is safe to eat. You'll also use it for bringing liquids up to a precise temperature when necessary.

Kitchen shears: Heavy-duty scissors that are particularly handy when breaking down poultry.

Mandoline: If your goal is extra thin and uniform slices, a mandoline is the way to go.

Mircroplane: For grating hard cheeses, spices, and garlic, as well as zesting citrus.

Oven thermometer: Ever follow a recipe exactly and have no idea why your cake came out upsettingly dry? Yeah, your oven temperature might be off. An oven thermometer makes sure you have the right temperature so you can be precise when it really matters.

Pasta paddle: It's optional, but it makes shaping gnocchi (see page 157) much simpler and more enjoyable.

Pasta roller: Again, optional. There are instructions to roll out and cut pasta by hand, but a roller is certainly faster.

Rice cooker: The name is self-explanatory. But in this book, I use it to make black garlic (see page 65). You don't need anything fancy.

Ricer: A ricer processes potatoes or other cooked foods through a sheet of tiny holes (each about the width of a grain of rice), kind of like a larger-scale garlic press. It's handy for achieving extra-smooth potatoes for gnocchi (page 157) or pomme puree (page 180).

Sauté pan: Exactly which type of pan you use depends on your preference. When it comes to searing meat and fish, carbon steel pans are my favorite by far. But cast iron and stainless steel are great, too.

Sharp knives: You've likely heard this before, but it's worth repeating: a sharp knife is safer than a dull knife. Not to mention, it will also make your job much easier.

Sous vide water circulator: For slow and precise cooking.

Stand mixer with a dough hook attachment: To make kneading dough (and bread making in general) a whole lot easier.

Tamis: A superfine-mesh strainer that can also be used in place of a food mill or ricer.

ICE BATH 101

I rely on ice baths to quickly cool down food. You don't need special equipment to create one. Simply fill a large bowl with ice and cold water. A metal bowl will chill faster if you have one!

A NOTE ABOUT KOSHER SALT

I call for kosher salt in most of my recipes. It's not as "salty" as table salt, and the grain size is larger. And yes, it can make a huge difference in the success of a dish—especially when it comes to fermentations and preserves. Iodized salt has a distinct flavor, and at higher percentages it can affect or even halt your fermentation.

When shopping for kosher salt, you'll most likely come across Diamond Crystal and Morton's, and my personal favorite is Diamond Crystal. Morton's kosher salt granules are larger and can lead to saltier results. Plus, they dissolve more slowly, which means that sometimes you're left with stubborn salt granules.

THE PANTRY

I THINK ONE OF THE MAIN DIFFERENCES BETWEEN THE BEST HOME COOKS AND RESTAURANT CHEFS COMES DOWN TO THEIR PANTRIES—THE PANTRY IS WHERE YOU'LL FIND THE BUILDING BLOCKS FOR A GOOD DISH. IF YOU WERE TO WALK INTO A RESTAURANT, YOU WOULD SEE A DRY STORAGE AND WALK-IN STOCKED WITH ALL KINDS OF DEHYDRATIONS, GARNISHES, AND CRUNCHIES. HAVING A NICE SELECTION IN YOUR PANTRY IS A GREAT WAY TO ELEVATE A DISH QUICKLY, WITH LOW EFFORT.

LIME LEAF PEANUTS

2 cups (251 grams) unsalted raw peanuts

7 fresh makrut lime leaves (see Note)

2 teaspoons ground coriander

2 teaspoons chili powder

2 teaspoons kosher salt

1 teaspoon ground ginger

SPECIAL EQUIPMENT:

food processor

In Southeast Asian cuisine, makrut lime leaves are used like bay leaves. Distinctly citrusy and bright, they can be added to any number of cooked dishes. When you remove the ribs from the leaves and blend the leafy parts, you get what I can only call lime leaf "floss," which works well to perfume dried foods. The possibilities for its use are endless. Here, I pulse the lime leaf floss with roasted peanuts, ground coriander, chili powder, and ground ginger for an aromatic and irresistible crunchy spice mix.

1 Preheat the oven to 350°F (177°C).

2 Spread the peanuts in an even layer in a half sheet pan. Roast for 15 to 20 minutes, until they turn golden and become fragrant. Spread on another sheet pan to cool.

3 Cut out and discard the center stems from the lime leaves—they're not edible. Place the leaves in the food processor and pulse until the leaves are mostly broken down and threadlike.

4 To the processor, add the toasted peanuts, then add the coriander, chili powder, salt, and ginger. Pulse until you have coarse crumbles roughly the same size.

5 Transfer the mixture to an airtight container and store at room temperature for up to 3 months or in the freezer for up to 1 year.

NOTE

You can buy makrut lime leaves fresh or frozen at most Asian grocery stores. They'll last indefinitely in the freezer.

BURNT ONION POWDER

2 large leeks

SPECIAL EQUIPMENT:
high-powered blender

Despite being burnt to a crisp, this powder retains the sweetness of an onion. You can boost vinaigrettes and pasta dough with this charred onion flavor. Or you can dust it over a finished dish, as in the Little Gems salad (page 135) to add a layer of complexity, not to mention a moody color.

1 Preheat the oven to 400°F (204°C).

2 Cut off and discard the roots and dark green tops of the leeks. Working with the white and pale green parts, cut each leek in half lengthwise, then separate the layers. Rinse the layers to remove any dirt, then pat them dry with a clean kitchen towel. It's important that the leeks be totally dry.

3 Fit a wire rack into a half sheet pan. Lay the leeks in a single layer on the rack. (If you need to use a couple of sheet pans, that's okay.) Roast 15 to 25 minutes, until leeks are completely dried out. The layers will vary slightly in darkness; parts of the leeks will be very dark brown, others blackened. If there are any spots that refuse to dry out and blacken, simply tear them off and discard.

4 Let the leeks cool completely. Add them to the blender and pulse until you have a fine powder. Transfer the powder to an airtight container and store at room temperature for up to 6 months.

GARLIC SCAPE POWDER

1 pound (454 grams)
   garlic scapes (see Note)

SPECIAL EQUIPMENT:

dehydrator, food
   processor, high-
   powered blender

Garlic scapes are the young, thin, curly stalks of hardneck garlic. Growers cut them off to concentrate energy in the growing bulbs. Often overlooked as an ingredient, scapes have a beautiful green color and mild garlicky flavor that's wonderful when dehydrated and dusted over a dish as a finishing touch.

1   If the garlic scapes have any flower buds, remove and discard them.

2   Rough chop the scapes into similarly sized pieces so they fit in the bowl of the food processor. Pulse a few times until you have a chunky, almost paste-like consistency.

3   Spread the paste in an even layer on the dehydrator tray and dry at 90°F (32°C) until completely dry, 8 to 12 hours.

4   Place the dried garlic scapes in the blender and pulse until you have a fine powder. Transfer the powder to an airtight container and store at room temperature for up to 1 year.

NOTE

Look for garlic scapes during late spring or early summer, usually at your local farmers' market.

ALL THE SEEDS MIX

¼ cup (45 grams) pepitas

¼ cup (35 grams) unsalted sunflower seeds

2 tablespoons flax seeds

2 tablespoons white sesame seeds

Kosher salt

SPECIAL EQUIPMENT:
food processor (optional)

This handy mix of seeds adds a good amount of flavor and texture to just about anything. Sprinkle it over roasted veggies or salads (like the Little Gems salad on page 135 or the Tomato and Peach Salad with Farmer Cheese and Dill Vinny salad on page 140), or use it as a crust on protein.

1   Preheat the oven to 350°F (177°C). Set the racks in the upper and lower thirds of the oven.

2   Spread the pepitas, sunflower seeds, and flax seeds in an even layer on a quarter sheet pan. Spread the sesame seeds on another quarter sheet pan in an even layer.

3   Place both sheet pans in the oven and toast the seeds, shaking and stirring halfway through, until the sesame seeds and sunflower seeds are light golden brown, about 8 minutes for the sesame seeds and 10 to 11 minutes for the pepita mixture.

4   Carefully spread the pepita mixture on another quarter sheet pan to stop the cooking. Spread the sesame seeds on a small plate to cool.

5   Place the cooled pepita mixture in a food processor. Add a pinch of salt and pulse until the seeds are all about the same size. (Alternatively, chop the pepita mixture, then mix in a pinch of salt.)

6   Transfer the pepita mixture to an airtight container, then add the sesame seeds. Store at room temperature for up to 3 months or in the freezer for up to 1 year.

LIME LEAF PEANUTS
(PAGE 26)

HAZELNUT CRUMBLE
(PAGE 33)

ALL THE SEEDS MIX
(PAGE 30)

PISTACHIO DUKKAH
(PAGE 32)

PISTACHIO DUKKAH

¾ cup (100 grams) unsalted raw pistachios

⅓ cup (45 grams) unsalted sunflower seeds

1 tablespoon white sesame seeds

2 teaspoons ground coriander

1 teaspoon ground cumin

1 teaspoon Aleppo pepper (see Note)

1 teaspoon flaky sea salt, such as Maldon

SPECIAL EQUIPMENT:

food processor (optional)

Dukkah (or duqqa) is an Egyptian seed and spice mix that is a great secret weapon in any pantry. Use it as a topping for salads, breads, and vegetables, or as a crust on things like lamb (check out page 188). It can also be eaten on its own as a snack.

1 Preheat the oven to 350°F (177°C).

2 Spread the pistachios, sunflower seeds, and sesame seeds separately on 3 sheet pans. Bake until all the seeds and nuts are toasted, about 8 minutes for the sesame seeds and 10 minutes for the pistachios and sunflower seeds. Let cool.

3 Place the pistachio and sunflower seeds in the food processor and pulse a few times until everything is about the same size but still chunky. (Alternatively, you can rough-chop by hand.) Transfer the mixture to a medium bowl.

4 Add the sesame seeds to the bowl along with the coriander, cumin, Aleppo pepper, and sea salt; toss to combine. Transfer the mixture to an airtight container and store at room temperature for up to 3 months or in the freezer for up to 1 year.

NOTE

Aleppo pepper has a more complex flavor than red pepper flakes. It's also not as spicy. These days, you can find it in big supermarket chains, but in a pinch, feel free to swap in red pepper flakes.

HAZELNUT CRUMBLE

1 cup (130 grams) raw hazelnuts

1 cup (85 grams) coriander seeds

3 limes

2 teaspoons kosher salt

SPECIAL EQUIPMENT:

food processor, Microplane or other zester

The combination of warm, earthy hazelnuts, lime zest, and floral, citrusy coriander makes for a great all-purpose garnish, perfect for salads, vegetables, seafood, and meat.

1 Preheat the oven to 350°F (177°C).

2 Place the hazelnuts in a quarter sheet pan and roast for 10 to 15 minutes, stirring halfway.

3 Immediately spread the warm hazelnuts on a clean kitchen towel. Fold the towel to cover the hazelnuts and let them steam for 2 minutes. Then, rub the hazelnuts with the towel—the skins should slip right off. Keep the oven turned on.

4 Spread the coriander seeds in the sheet pan and roast for 3 to 4 minutes, until they have darkened to a nice deep brown. Transfer the seeds to a plate to cool.

5 Using a Microplane, grate the zest from the limes.

6 When the nuts and seeds are cool, add the coriander seeds to the food processor and pulse until they're mostly broken down. Add the hazelnuts, then the lime zest and the salt. Pulse again until everything is about the same size.

7 Transfer the mixture to an airtight container and store at room temperature for up to 3 months.

BLACK LIMES

5 limes

2 teaspoons kosher salt

SPECIAL EQUIPMENT:

dehydrator, food
  processor (optional),
  Microplane or other
  grater (optional)

Tangy with a musky citrus flavor, black limes are associated with numerous Middle Eastern cuisines. Because they're almost indefinitely shelf stable, they are really handy to have around when you want to add a quick punch of citrus. Grind them into a powder to add to spice mixes and rubs. Or grate them over soups, seafood dishes, or even drinks (as for my Honeydew and Verjus with Ginger and Black Lime drink, page 239).

1   Prepare an ice bath in a large bowl.

2   Place the limes in a medium saucepan and add water to cover. Add the salt, then bring to a boil over high heat and cook for 1 minute. This boiling will remove any bitterness from the peel.

3   Scoop out the limes and transfer them to the ice bath. Let sit until completely cool, 2 to 3 minutes. Take out the limes and dry them.

4   Place the limes on a dehydrator tray and dehydrate at 160°F (71°C) until black, lighter in weight, and very hard, 3 to 5 days. If the limes have seeds, you might even hear them rattling around when you give the limes a shake.

5   If desired, grind the limes into a powder in the food processor, but make sure you remove the seeds first. Or, keep the limes whole and enjoy grating them over dishes with a Microplane or other citrus grater.

6   Transfer the dried limes (or lime powder) to an airtight container and store at room temperature for years or in the freezer indefinitely.

POTATO CRUMBS

1 large russet potato

2 cups (473 milliliters) neutral oil, such as sunflower, grapeseed, or vegetable

Kosher salt

SPECIAL EQUIPMENT:

high-powered blender, instant-read thermometer

These potato crumbs make a great crispy garnish, but you can also use them as a breading of sorts. Think potato panko. Roll whatever you feel like eating in the potato flakes and then fry away. The taste of potato chips is sure to both confuse and delight whomever you're cooking for, and witnessing this spectacle is the best part.

1   Scrub the outside of the potato with a vegetable brush. Cut the potato into 8 equal pieces—they don't need to be perfect.

2   Transfer the potato pieces to the blender and add just enough water to cover. (Too little water and it will puree; too much water and it simply won't work.) Pulse 3 or 4 times, until the potato looks like panko. If the pieces are still a little too large, pulse a few more times.

3   Line a mesh strainer with a clean kitchen towel, then drain the potato crumbs, catching the water in a bowl below. Wring and squeeze as much water out of the crumbs and the cloth as you can. Spread the potato crumbs on a half sheet pan to dry for about 15 minutes.

4   Place the oil in a large, deep pot and heat over medium-low heat until it reaches 350°F (177°C). Place another pot (or bain marie) alongside, and ready a mesh strainer to strain the hot oil. Line a half sheet pan with a paper towel for draining the fried potatoes.

5   When the oil comes to 350°F (177°C), add a couple tablespoons of the crumbs to see how they react. They should immediately bubble. Dividing the crumbs into 3 or 4 batches, fry each batch of potato crumbs for 2 to 3 minutes, until they begin to turn golden brown. They will continue to darken as they sit in the oil, so pull them out before they are dark brown or they will burn. (Do not put all the potato crumbs in the oil at once or it will bubble over and be a huge mess.)

6   Strain the fried crumbs as they finish cooking, and lay them on the sheet pan to drain. Immediately season with the salt and let cool completely.

7   Repeat with the remaining potato crumbs, making sure the oil is at temperature before adding the next batch.

8   Transfer the cooled crumbs to an airtight container and store at room temperature for up to 5 days.

SALT AND VINEGAR POWDER

¼ cup (30 grams) kosher salt

¼ cup (30 grams) white vinegar powder (see Note)

SPECIAL EQUIPMENT:

high-powered blender

This recipe comes together in less than 5 minutes with only 2 ingredients. It's also incredibly versatile. You can use the familiar, fun flavor on staples like chips or fries, but I also like it in unexpected places, like on fried pig ears, chicharrons, fried sweetbreads, and Puffed Beef Tendon (page 96).

1   Place the salt in the blender and blend on high until you have a fine powder. Add the vinegar powder and pulse until thoroughly mixed.

2   Transfer the powder to an airtight container and store at room temperature indefinitely. To use, place some of the powder in a spice shaker to dust over everything.

NOTE

White vinegar powder is a dehydrated form of standard white vinegar. Don't worry if you haven't seen this powder in your grocery store; it's easy to source online. Beyond blending it with salt to make a delicious snack dust, you can use it to enliven dressings, marinades, or sauces.

HOT SAUCE POWDER

¼ cup (30 grams) kosher salt

2 tablespoons Aleppo pepper (see Note on page 32)

1 tablespoon garlic powder

2 teaspoons paprika

¼ cup (30 grams) white vinegar powder (see Note on page 39)

SPECIAL EQUIPMENT:

high-powered blender

Building on the classic salt-and-vinegar flavor profile, I add traditional ingredients you'd see in a vinegar-based hot sauce. You can use this spice mix in the same fashion as you would the Salt and Vinegar Powder (page 39), and you can't go wrong with it on popcorn or chips. But dusting it over fried chicken is my favorite way to use it. Irresistible hot-sauce flavor, zero sogginess.

1 Add the salt, Aleppo pepper, garlic powder, and paprika to the blender and blend on high until you have a fine powder. Add the vinegar powder and pulse until thoroughly mixed.

2 Transfer the powder to an airtight container and store at room temperature for up to 6 months. To use, place some of the powder in a spice shaker to dust over everything.

PUFFED GRAINS

2 tablespoons whole-grain sorghum

Kosher salt

1 tablespoon whole-grain amaranth

1 tablespoon red quinoa

1 tablespoon wild rice

Neutral oil, such as sunflower, grapeseed, or vegetable

SPECIAL EQUIPMENT:

instant-read thermometer

You can pop all sorts of grains besides corn. This toasty mix is great for bulking things up and making them look fluffy. Make my Shishitos with Bonito Aioli and Puffed Grains (page 115) and you'll get it. While this works well for savory applications, it's surprisingly great for desserts, too. Sprinkle the puffed grains over chocolate mousse and you'll have no regrets.

1   Heat a small sauté pan (or shallow straight-sided pan) that has a lid over medium heat for 2 minutes. Add the sorghum, then cover with the lid. Cook about 3 minutes, shaking the pan every few seconds so it doesn't burn, until the popping stops. Transfer the puffed sorghum to a quarter sheet pan and season with the salt. Let cool.

2   Return the pan to medium heat. Add the amaranth and cover again with the lid. Cook about 1 minute, shaking the pan every few seconds, until the popping stops or the amaranth starts to darken. (Some grains may not pop.) Transfer the puffed amaranth to the sheet pan and season with the salt. Let cool.

3   Return the pan to medium heat. Add the quinoa and cover again with the lid. Cook about 1 minute, shaking the pan every few seconds, until the popping stops or the quinoa starts to darken. (Some may not pop.) Transfer the puffed quinoa to the sheet pan and season with the salt. Let cool.

4   Add enough of the oil to the pan so that it is about ¼ inch deep. Heat the oil to 350°F (177°C). Place another pot and a strainer nearby. Line a small sheet pan with paper towels.

5   When the oil comes to temperature, add the wild rice. As soon as it puffs up, immediately strain the rice and transfer it to the sheet pan. Season with the salt and let cool.

6   When everything has cooled, mix the puffed grains well. Transfer to an airtight container and store at room temperature for up to 1 week.

PICKLES, FERMENTATIONS, AND PRESERVES

AN EXTENSION OF YOUR PANTRY. MOST OF THE RECIPES IN THIS CHAPTER ARE PRETTY HANDS-OFF AND WILL LAST FOR QUITE A WHILE IN YOUR FRIDGE.

CALIFORNIA KOSHO

20 Meyer lemons
2 fresh serrano chiles
Kosher salt

SPECIAL EQUIPMENT:

high-powered blender, Microplane or other zester, digital scale, fermentation lid (optional; see Note)

Yuzu kosho is a Japanese condiment made from fermented yuzu peels and chiles. Spicy, tangy, and a little bitter, it's amazing. Fresh yuzu is hard to find stateside, which means it's also very expensive. But when we apply the same method to Meyer lemons, a local, abundant, and similar type of fruit, we can create something just as tasty.

1   *Option 1:* Rinse, clean, and peel the lemons. If there's any thick white pith on any of the peels, trim it off. Place the lemon peels in the blender and pulse, scraping down the sides with a rubber spatula as needed, until you have a fairly smooth paste.

Option 2: Rinse and clean the lemons, then zest them with the Microplane onto a cutting board. Run a knife through the lemon zest until you have a fairly smooth paste.

2   Set a medium bowl on a digital scale, then set the scale to zero by pressing the Tare button. Remove the bowl from the scale, then transfer the lemon peel paste to the bowl.

3   Finely chop the serrano chiles, including the seeds. Add to the bowl with the lemon peel paste. Add the juice from 1 lemon. Stir to combine.

4   Return the bowl to the scale and weigh the mixture in grams. Using this weight, add 10 percent of that weight in kosher salt. (For example, if your paste weighs 200 grams, add 20 grams of kosher salt.) Stir the salt into the paste, then transfer to a 1-cup glass jar. Label and date the jar, then cover with the fermentation lid.

5   Set the jar aside at room temperature, away from direct sunlight, for 14 days to ferment. (Placing in a cupboard is ideal, as it's out of the way.)

6   When ready, replace the fermentation lid with an airtight lid and store the jar in the fridge for up to 6 months.

NOTE

I recommend a fermentation lid here because it has a small valve that allows gas to escape without opening the jar. If you don't have one, no worries. You'll just need to open the jar to "burp" it every other day.

CA. Kosho 8/15/22

PRESERVED LEMONS

8 to 10 Meyer lemons

½ cup (90 grams) kosher salt

SPECIAL EQUIPMENT:

fermentation lid (optional; see Note on page 18)

I always have preserved lemons in my kitchen—probably because I grew up in California, where it felt like *everyone* had a lemon tree in their yard. This technique of packing lemons and salt into a jar originated in Morocco, and it couldn't be easier. You basically let time do all the work. As the lemons sit, the peels soften and take on uniquely salty, acidic, and floral flavors that pair especially well with seafood. The lemon peels can be cut into strips, diced up, or blended (see Preserved Lemon Gel on page 52). As for the brine, use it for drinks or vinaigrettes (see Preserved Lemon Vinaigrette, page 74).

1   Rinse and clean the lemons. As though you were cutting the lemons into quarters, cut through the lemons from the top to within ½ inch of the base, keeping the quarters connected.

2   Add 1 tablespoon of the salt to a 1-quart glass jar, then add the rest of the salt to a large bowl. Rub the insides of each of the quartered lemons with the salt in the bowl.

3   Add 1 lemon to the jar. Tamp down on the lemon, squeezing out as much juice as you can, then add a pinch of salt from the bowl. Repeat until all the lemons are tightly packed and submerged under salty lemon juice. Add any remaining salt to the jar. If your lemons aren't submerged in juice, squeeze some fresh lemon juice over the top.

4   Label and date the jar, then cover it with the fermentation lid. Set the jar aside at room temperature, away from sunlight, for up to 30 days. Every few days, gently shake the jar to redistribute any sediment and to resubmerge the lemons under the juice.

5   Start to check the lemons after 2 weeks to see if they're done. You will know they are ready when the peels are soft, tender, and very fragrant. If your lemons are mushy, you went too long. Store the jar in the fridge for up to 6 months.

PRESERVED LEMON GEL

1 quart (800 grams)
Preserved Lemons
(page 51)

1½ cups (300 grams)
granulated sugar

¾ cup (177 milliliters)
water

1 teaspoon ground
turmeric

SPECIAL EQUIPMENT:

high-powered blender

Citrus contains a gelling agent called pectin, and with pectin comes power. Armed with that knowledge, you can quite easily make a fancy-looking gel as impressive and delicious as one you'd see in a fine restaurant. Using preserved lemons takes everything to the next level.

1   Remove the seeds from the preserved lemons, leaving the rest of the lemon intact.

2   Add the sugar and water to a medium saucepan over medium heat. Warm until the sugar dissolves, about 3 minutes.

3   Add the lemons and bring to a boil; that should take about 2 minutes. When it comes to a boil, transfer the mixture to the blender; add the turmeric. Blend until the mixture has thickened and is smooth and shiny.

4   Transfer to a 1-quart glass jar or airtight container and add a label with the date. Store in the fridge for up to 1 year.

PICKLED RED ONIONS

3 small red onions

2 garlic cloves

10 coriander seeds

5 black peppercorns

1½ cups (375 milliliters) water

1½ cups (375 milliliters) Champagne vinegar

¼ cup (50 grams) granulated sugar

1 tablespoon kosher salt

Pickled red onions are so common and popular that when deciding whether to include this recipe in the book, I thought, *Does the world really need another recipe?* But then I remembered cutting 60 onions to make huge batches of this very recipe because—you know what? They're pretty nice to have around. With a vibrant color and bright flavor, you can add these pickled red onions to most things, be it sauce or salad. So here they are in the book.

1   Slice the onions in half from top to bottom, then julienne or cut into ¼-inch-thick strips. Smash the garlic.

2   Pack the onions tightly into a 1-quart glass jar along with the garlic.

3   Place the coriander seeds and peppercorns in a small saucepan over medium-low heat and gently toast for about 3 minutes, until fragrant.

4   Add the water, vinegar, sugar, and salt. Increase the heat to medium-high and bring to a boil. When the mixture reaches a boil, immediately pour it over the onions. Let cool to room temperature.

5   Cover the jar and store in the fridge for up to 3 weeks, ideally waiting at least 1 day until you use them.

PEAR MOSTARDA

1 pound (454 grams) firm Anjou pears

2 cups (402 grams) granulated sugar

1 teaspoon brown mustard seeds

1 teaspoon yellow mustard seeds

SPECIAL EQUIPMENT:

instant-read thermometer

Mostarda di frutta hails from the northern part of Italy. It's a delicious way to preserve fruit and is a common accompaniment to cheese and cured meats. I really like it on a piece of toast with ricotta. Or, with a perfectly seared pork chop with some fennel pollen (see page 192). For this method, it's best to use fairly firm pears. The preserving process will soften the pears quite a bit, so if they're already pretty ripe, they'll break down too much and will disappear. When picking your pears, gently poke the neck of the pear with your finger. If there's any give, it's probably close to being too ripe. If it's firm, it's good to go for this application.

When I made this in restaurants, we'd omit the mustard seeds and add that flavor later, with just a couple drops of mustard seed oil. (Yandilla brand was our go-to.) Doing it this way allowed us to use the wonderful pear syrup for other recipes, or to give it to the bar to use for some dope cocktails.

1   Peel the pears and cut them in half from top to bottom. Use a spoon to scoop out the core and seeds. Pour enough sugar into an 8-inch square baking dish to cover the bottom, then lay the pears cut side down on top of the sugar. Pour the rest of the sugar on top, then cover the dish with plastic wrap. Leave it somewhere cool and out of sunlight for 24 hours.

2   The next day, the sugar should be mostly dissolved. Transfer the sugar syrup and any undissolved sugar to a large saucepan. Set the heat to low and add the brown and yellow mustard seeds. When the sugar has dissolved, add the halved pears.

3   Cook the pears and syrup until the syrup reaches 223°F (102°C), or thread stage.

4   Remove the saucepan from the heat and cool completely. Transfer the pears and syrup to an airtight container or jar and store in the fridge for up to 3 months.

CHERRY MOSTARDA

1 pound (454 grams)
fresh cherries, any kind

1¼ cups (250 grams)
granulated sugar

1½ teaspoons yellow
mustard seeds

1½ teaspoons brown
mustard seeds

1 teaspoon ascorbic acid
(see Note)

Kosher salt

Here's another version of mostarda, with a slightly different approach. With some fruits, it's better to heat up the sugar syrup pulled from the fruit itself, then pour it back over the fruit to preserve the texture. This method turns cherries into little chewy bites, kind of like gummy candy.

1 Remove the pits from the cherries. If you own a cherry pitter, great; if not, a metal straw will do the job well—simply push the pits out.

2 Cut the cherries in half and place them in an airtight container. Add the sugar and give it a shake. Leave the container at room temperature for 24 hours.

3 The next day, a lot of liquid should have been pulled out of the fruit and the sugar should be almost fully dissolved. If not, shake the container until it's completely dissolved.

4 Strain the syrup into a small saucepan and bring it to a boil over medium-high heat. When the syrup reaches a boil, pour it over the cherries in the container. Let cool completely, then place the container in the fridge overnight.

5 The next day, repeat the process of straining off the syrup, bringing it to a boil, and pouring it back over the cherries. Let cool completely, then place in the fridge overnight.

6 On the third day, strain the syrup into a small pot and add the yellow and brown mustard seeds and the ascorbic acid. Bring to a boil over medium-high heat, then immediately pour over the cherries one final time. Let cool completely.

7 Store the container in the fridge for up to 3 months.

NOTE

Ascorbic acid is also referred to as vitamin C powder, and like most such ingredients, it can be purchased online. Just a little bit of the pucker-inducing ingredient helps to preserve the cherries. You can also use it to prepare acidulated water (see page 195).

SWEET PICKLED SHALLOTS

4 small shallots

½ cup (125 milliliters) water

½ cup (125 milliliters) Champagne vinegar

½ cup (90 grams) granulated sugar

1 teaspoon kosher salt

I think shallots deserve a little more hype. Because they're milder and more delicate than onions, these pickled shallots add just the right amount of acid and savory onion flavor, without overpowering anything. They're my go-to when it comes to starters like smoked fish dip and gravlax.

1   Peel and slice the shallots into ¼-inch-thick rings. Pack into a 1-pint glass jar.

2   Combine the water, vinegar, sugar, and salt in a small pot. Bring to a boil over medium-high heat, then immediately pour it over the shallots. Let cool to room temperature.

3   Cover the jar and store in the fridge for up to 7 days.

SAUERKRAUT

1 large head of green cabbage

2 tablespoons kosher salt

10 coriander seeds

10 caraway seeds

5 black peppercorns

SPECIAL EQUIPMENT:

digital scale, fermentation weight (optional), fermentation lid (optional; see Note on page 18)

Sauerkraut is by far the easiest and most predictable ingredient to ferment. If you've never fermented anything (intentionally, lol), start with this recipe—the gateway fermentation. There are many ways to fancy it up, but for sauerkraut's most basic form, all you need is cabbage and salt. Most fermentations use a set percentage of salt to control the speed of fermentation, the texture, and the bacteria. This fermentation is a 2 percent salt ferment. For precision and ease, I highly recommend using a scale.

1 Cut the cabbage into quarters through the base, then remove the core from each quarter. Slice the cabbage into about ¼-inch-thick slices.

2 Set a large bowl on a digital scale, then set to zero by pressing the Tare button. Add the cabbage to the bowl and weigh the cabbage in grams. Using this weight, add 2 percent of that weight in salt. (For example, if your cabbage is 900 grams, that's 18 grams of salt.)

3 Massage the salt into the cabbage and leave the bowl out on the counter for 1 hour. Come back and massage the cabbage again. Begin to squeeze out the liquid from the cabbage. Leave it out on the counter for 1 hour more. When you're ready to move on to the next step, there should be quite a bit of liquid in the bowl—this is the brine you'll use to ferment the cabbage.

4 If you're using a 1-quart glass jar, wrap the coriander seeds, caraway seeds, and black peppercorns in a small square of cheesecloth and tie with some kitchen twine. (If you're using a couple of pint jars, divide the spices between 2 squares of cheesecloth.) Place the cheesecloth packet in the bottom of the jar. Pack the cabbage into the jar with the brine, leaving about 1 inch of headroom and making sure the cabbage is submerged. I recommend using a fermentation weight on top to keep the cabbage submerged.

5 Label and date the jar, then cover it with a fermentation lid. Leave the jar somewhere cool for 2 weeks—about 60°F (15°C) is ideal. If this is your first fermentation, taste the cabbage every few days so you can see what's happening.

6 When the sauerkraut is ready, replace the fermentation lid with an airtight lid and store in the fridge for up to 4 months.

FERMENTED RADISH

1 large bunch Purple Ninja radishes (or Purple Daikon)

2 small shallots

2¼ cups (530 milliliters) water

1 tablespoon plus 2 teaspoons kosher salt

SPECIAL EQUIPMENT:

digital scale, fermentation weight, fermentation lid (optional; see Note on page 18)

As for most fermentations, here I use a percentage of salt based on the total weight of the ingredients. This is an example of a 2 percent salt application. If you wish to scale this recipe up or down to work with the specific amount of radish you have, just weigh the radish and water, and determine 2 percent of that total. That's how much salt you'll need.

To get this bright pink shade on the fermented radish I use Purple Ninja radishes, which are purple inside. You can use any radish you want, but the color won't be the same.

1   Remove any of the greens still attached to the radishes. Thoroughly wash the radishes with a vegetable brush. If the radishes are large, cut them in half. Peel and halve the shallots.

2   Set a 1-quart glass jar on a digital scale, then set to zero by pressing the Tare button. Add the radishes and shallots, then pour over enough water to cover the radishes, leaving at least 1 inch of headroom. Weigh the radishes, shallots, and water in grams, then figure 2 percent of that weight for the kosher salt. (For example, if your radishes weigh 400 grams, that's 8 grams of kosher salt.) Don't add the salt yet.

3   Pour the water into a large bowl. Add the salt to the water and stir to dissolve, then pour the water into the jar.

4   Add a fermentation weight to keep the radishes submerged. Cover with a fermentation lid and leave at room temperature out of direct sunlight for 7 to 14 days. The longer you leave the jar out, the more acidic and funky the radishes will be. They'll also get softer. My sweet spot is 10 days.

5   When the radishes are ready, replace the fermentation lid with an airtight lid and store the jar in the fridge for up to 3 months.

BLACK GARLIC

2 bulbs of garlic (see Note)

SPECIAL EQUIPMENT:
rice cooker or dehydrator

At first glance, this garlic appears to be burnt, but I promise it's anything but bitter. The slowly cooked and fermented cloves bring a sweetness similar to garlic confit. But because of the Maillard reaction (which causes browning in cooking), they also pack a punch of umami. Here, I've listed two different ways to make this. Just note that whichever route you decide to take, it *will* make your home smell of garlic. For this reason, placing the rice cooker or dehydrator on a covered patio or in a garage is common practice.

METHOD 1: RICE COOKER (30 DAYS AHEAD)

1 Trim the root end of the garlic bulbs, keeping the cloves together. Peel away any loose skin on the outside, exposing clean, tightly wrapped garlic cloves.

2 Wrap each bulb tightly in a piece of aluminum foil. Transfer to the bowl of the rice cooker. Set the rice cooker to the Warm setting and let the garlic cook until the cloves are black, moist, and a little sticky, about 30 days. Start checking at 21 days. To check if the garlic is ready, cut off the top of a bulb. If it's light brown, give it an additional week to cook until black.

3 Place the garlic in an airtight container and store in the fridge for up to 6 months or freeze for up to 1 year.

METHOD 2: DEHYDRATOR (3 WEEKS AHEAD)

1 Trim the root of the garlic bulbs, keeping the cloves together. Peel away any loose skin on the outside, exposing clean, tightly wrapped garlic cloves.

2 Wrap each bulb tightly in plastic wrap, then in aluminum foil. Transfer to a rack in the dehydrator. Set the dehydrator to 130°F (55°C) and let dry until the cloves are black, moist, and a little sticky, about 3 weeks. To check if the garlic is ready, cut off the top of a bulb. If it's light brown, give it an additional week until the color is black.

3 Place the garlic in an airtight container and store in the fridge for up to 6 months or in the freezer for up to 1 year.

NOTE

Since each bulb of garlic is wrapped individually, you can easily scale this recipe up or down.

CURED EGG YOLKS

¾ cup (100 grams)
kosher salt

½ cup (100 grams)
granulated sugar

6 large eggs

SPECIAL EQUIPMENT:

dehydrator

After they're cured, egg yolks take on a flavor that I can only describe as savory. They retain that eggy flavor you expect, but also with a punch of umami and saltiness. Use them as a topping to level up dishes that traditionally have an egg—such as shaved over a tartare, pasta, or rice dish.

1   In a large bowl, combine the salt and sugar. Add about half the mixture to a nonreactive container large enough to fit 6 yolks. Use the back of a tablespoon or the bottom of an egg to make little wells in the mixture to mark where the yolks will sit, making sure you don't expose the bottom of the container.

2   Working one at a time, separate the egg yolks from the whites, then gently lay the yolks in the wells. (Reserve the egg whites for another use.)

3   Cover the egg yolks with the rest of the salt mixture so they are no longer visible. Cover the container and refrigerate for 4 days.

4   Remove the yolks from the salt mixture, brushing off any excess salt. The yolks should now be bright orange and translucent. (If the salt doesn't come off easily, give the yolks a quick rinse under running water.)

5   Place the yolks on a dehydrator tray and dry at 150°F (65°C) for 2 hours, until they are opaque and feel like a semi-firm cheese.

6   Transfer the cured yolks to an airtight container and store in the fridge for up to 3 months.

VINAIGRETTES AND DRESSINGS

NEVER UNDERESTIMATE THE POWER OF A GOOD VINAIGRETTE. THESE NEXT-LEVEL DRESSINGS MAKE SALADS AND VEGETABLES ANYTHING BUT BORING.

FINE HERB VINAIGRETTE

1¼ cups (296 milliliters) sunflower oil

1 small bunch fresh chives

¼ large bunch fresh parsley

¼ large bunch fresh tarragon, leaves only

¼ large bunch fresh chervil

Kosher salt

1 tablespoon sherry vinegar

SPECIAL EQUIPMENT:

high-powered blender

This recipe takes the classic French herb blend and turns it into a light and refreshing dressing perfect for salads, toast, or seafood. Why place the oil in the freezer prior to blending? Because blenders cause friction, which results in heat. To retain the bright flavors, you don't want to inadvertently "cook" the herbs in this recipe.

1   Place the sunflower oil in the freezer for 1 hour prior to blending.

2   Add the sunflower oil, all the herbs, and a pinch of salt to the blender. Blend until smooth, not letting the oil get warm. Stir in the vinegar. Taste and add more salt and a splash more of vinegar, if needed.

3   Transfer to an airtight container and store in the fridge for up to 1 week or freezer for up to 3 months.

CHARRED ONION VINAIGRETTE

2 cups (473 milliliters)
Charred Onion Broth
(page 89)

½ cup (125 milliliters)
extra-virgin olive oil

2 tablespoons fresh lime
juice

1 teaspoon sherry
vinegar

1 teaspoon soy sauce

Kosher salt and freshly
ground black pepper

The dark yet sweet flavor of this vinaigrette pairs well with grilled meats. A grilled rib eye served with a mountain of bright herbs dressed with this? Heaven.

1 Place the stock in a small saucepan over medium heat and boil to reduce until the color is black and the flavor is intense. You'll need ¾ cup of liquid for this recipe. Let cool to room temperature.

2 Transfer the reduced stock to a medium squeeze bottle. Add the olive oil, lime juice, vinegar, and soy sauce. Season to taste with salt and pepper.

3 Cover and store in the fridge for up to 1 week. Shake well before using to dress greens.

PRESERVED LEMON VINAIGRETTE

¼ cup (50 milliliters) juice from Preserved Lemons (page 51)

¼ cup (50 milliliters) fresh lemon juice

2 tablespoons honey or brown rice syrup

⅔ cup (158 milliliters) lemon-infused olive oil

Kosher salt and freshly ground black pepper

When you've used your entire jar of preserved lemons, don't throw out the juice! Highly acidic, floral, and with just the right salty flavor, the juice is a wonderful addition to vinaigrettes and sauces.

1 Combine the juice from the preserved lemons, the fresh lemon juice, and honey in a small bowl. Whisk until the honey is fully dissolved. Whisk in the olive oil until the vinaigrette is emulsified. Season to taste with salt and pepper.

2 Store in an airtight container in the fridge for up to 1 week.

SHALLOT, SHERRY, AND WALNUT DRESSING

4 small shallots

½ cup (125 milliliters) sunflower oil

½ cup (50 grams) walnuts

3 tablespoons sherry vinegar

2 tablespoons Dijon mustard

2 tablespoons water

½ cup (125 milliliters) extra-virgin olive oil

Kosher salt and freshly ground black pepper

SPECIAL EQUIPMENT:

high-powered blender

This creamy, but highly acidic dressing is thickened with walnuts, making it ideal for large leaf or wedge salads. Incidentally, it's also vegan.

1   Peel each shallot and trim the root end. Cut each in half lengthwise to expose a large surface.

2   Heat a large sauté pan (or shallow straight-sided pan) over medium-low heat and add the sunflower oil. Add the shallots cut side down and slowly caramelize. After about 4 minutes, give them a flip and caramelize the other sides, another 3 to 4 minutes. The shallots should be nicely browned on both sides and very soft. Remove the shallots from the oil, then pour out the oil and reserve. Let cool.

3   To the same pan, add the walnuts and toast them, shaking occasionally, until they are slightly darkened, about 3 minutes. Remove and let cool.

4   Place the vinegar, mustard, water, the caramelized shallots, and the toasted walnuts in the blender. Blend until completely smooth, scraping down the sides as needed. Slowly stream in the reserved sunflower oil until fully incorporated. Then stream in the olive oil and blend until emulsified.

5   Season to taste with salt and pepper. Store in an airtight container in the fridge for up to 1 week.

STOCKS AND SAUCES

A SAUCE CAN MAKE OR BREAK A DISH, AND AT THE FOUNDATION OF MOST GOOD SAUCES IS A HOMEMADE STOCK. WHILE STORE-BOUGHT CARTONS OF STOCK CAN BE CONVENIENT FOR A QUICK MEAL, YOU'RE GOING TO WANT TO SKIP THEM WHEN COOKING THE RECIPES IN THIS BOOK—THEIR ADDED SALTS, SUGARS, AND COLORINGS YIELD SOMETHING THAT TASTES ENTIRELY DIFFER-ENT FROM WHAT HAS BEEN INTENDED HERE. AND MAKING STOCK YOURSELF IS A GREAT WAY TO USE UP ANY SCRAPS YOU MAY HAVE LYING AROUND. FOR INSTANCE, I LIKE TO SAVE CHICKEN BONES IN THE FREEZER UNTIL I HAVE ENOUGH TO MAKE SOME STOCK.

CHILE POMODORO

1 fresh medium Fresno chile

15 garlic cloves

¼ cup (59 milliliters) extra-virgin olive oil

1 28-ounce can San Marzano tomatoes (no need to drain; these are usually canned with tomato puree, so just use it)

Leaves of 1 bunch fresh basil

Kosher salt

Sometimes the best recipes have the fewest ingredients. Canned tomatoes (they're picked and preserved at the peak of their season!), quality olive oil, a ton of garlic, a fresh chile, and fresh herbs—that's all you need to make a good sauce. It's simplicity, elevated.

1   Slice the chile into ¼-inch slices and thinly slice the garlic.

2   Heat the olive oil in a large saucepan over medium-low heat. Add the chile and cook, stirring occasionally, for 1 minute. Reduce the heat to low and add the garlic. Cook the garlic about 2 minutes, stirring occasionally, until it begins to turn golden and fragrant.

3   Add the tomatoes and use a spatula or wooden spoon to lightly crush them. Simmer, stirring occasionally, for 20 minutes. Add the basil and cook until the sauce has thickened, another 15 minutes.

4   Taste and adjust the seasoning to taste with the salt. Use immediately or let cool completely before transferring to an airtight container. Store in the fridge for up to 1 week.

BROWN BUTTER EMULSION

½ cup (1 stick; 115 grams) unsalted butter

½ cup (50 grams) dry milk powder

1 orange

3 to 4 lemons

Kosher salt

SPECIAL EQUIPMENT:
high-powered blender

The secret ingredient in this sauce is milk powder, which reinforces the brown butter with additional milk solids. With the acid from the lemon juice, the bitterness of the peel, and a pinch of salt, it's nicely balanced. I like to pair it with seafood, particularly pan-seared fish or scallops (see page 195).

1 Place the butter in a medium saucepan and heat gently over medium-low heat until melted. Stir in the milk powder. Cook for about 4 minutes, stirring constantly, until the milk solids are light golden brown. Remove from the heat and let cool to room temperature.

2 Using a vegetable peeler, peel a strip of orange peel and a strip of lemon peel.

3 Juice enough lemons to yield ¾ cup (170 milliliters) of juice. Add the lemon juice to the browned butter.

4 Transfer the butter mixture to the blender along with a pinch of salt, the orange peel, and the lemon peel and blend until smooth. Season to taste. Cover and keep warm until serving.

BEEF STOCK

2 large yellow onions

5 pounds (2.2 kilograms) beef bones, neck, and knuckle

Neutral oil, such as sunflower, grapeseed, or vegetable

2 tablespoons tomato paste

5 celery ribs

3 large carrots

10 fresh thyme sprigs

10 black peppercorns

1 fresh bay leaf (or 2 dried)

SPECIAL EQUIPMENT:

instant-read thermometer

This beef stock is the backbone of many of my reductions. I like to use bones that contain some marrow and a bit of meat. Marrow is high in collagen, which turns into gelatin and adds rich body to the sauce; the meat adds some additional flavor.

1 Preheat the oven to 450°F (232°C). Fit a wire rack into a half sheet pan.

2 Slice 1 yellow onion into ½-inch-thick rings. Heat a large skillet over high heat until it just starts to smoke. Place the onion rings in the pan and blacken on one side; this is an onion brûlée. It will add richness in both color and flavor to the stock.

3 Place the bones in a large bowl and lightly dress in oil. Arrange the bones on the rack, then place in the oven. Roast for 25 minutes, or until the bones are deep brown. Carefully spread the tomato paste on the hot bones and return the rack to the oven for an additional 5 minutes, until the tomato paste is a deep brick red. Transfer the bones to a large bowl or plate. Keep the oven rack and sheet pan handy. Keep the oven on.

4 While the bones are roasting, roughly chop the remaining onion, the celery, and carrots (your mirepoix) into similarly sized pieces (mirepoix cut). Dress the vegetables lightly with some oil and add to the rack in the sheet pan. Roast for 15 minutes, until the vegetables have some color to them. Remove to a bowl. (Even though the mirepoix isn't added until later, I recommend doing this step in tandem with the bones to save some time.)

5 Place the roasted bones in a stockpot and cover with water. Bring to a boil over high heat, then drop the heat to low and gently simmer for 3 hours. Skim any foam that rises to the top—this is congealed protein that will make your stock cloudy and slightly alter the flavor. The ideal temperature to simmer the stock is around 205°F (96°C). Visually, there should be just a couple bubbles rising ever so gently as it cooks.

6 Add the mirepoix, the thyme, peppercorns, and bay leaf. Simmer for an additional 3 hours.

7 Prepare an ice bath in a large bowl. Scoop out the bones and vegetables from the stock, then strain the liquid through a fine-mesh strainer into a large bowl. Place that bowl in the ice bath to cool the liquid quickly. (See Note about what to do with the bones.)

8 Transfer the stock to airtight containers and store in the fridge for up to 5 days or in the freezer for up to 3 months.

NOTE

An optional step, which I highly encourage, is to place the cooked bones back in the stockpot, cover them with fresh water, and simmer them again for a few hours more. This is called a remouillage, or "second stock." It is weaker in flavor and can be saved in the freezer to start your next batch of stock, or it can be reduced and added to your current stock.

BLOND CHICKEN STOCK

1 pound (454 grams) chicken feet

1 pound (454 grams) chicken backs

1 large yellow onion

2 large carrots

2 celery ribs

10 fresh thyme sprigs

10 black peppercorns

1 fresh bay leaf (or 2 dried)

SPECIAL EQUIPMENT:

instant-read thermometer

The difference between a blond and a brown stock is slight in terms of process, but the flavor gap is huge. Blond stock does not involve any roasting; instead, the bones are blanched and rinsed, which allows most of the impurities to rise to the surface to be poured off. Whereas brown stock is deeper in color and richer in flavor, blond stock is lighter and more neutral. I use this blond stock a lot for soups, rice dishes, and pastas—anytime I don't want chicken to be the primary flavor.

1   Place the chicken feet and backs in a stockpot and cover with water. Bring to a boil over high heat, then drop the heat to medium or medium-low and gently simmer for 15 minutes.

2   Meanwhile, roughly chop the onion, carrots, and celery (the mirepoix) into similarly sized pieces (mirepoix cut).

3   Strain out the chicken parts and drain the water from the pot. Rinse the pot well. Place the chicken back in the pot and cover with fresh water.

4   Once again, bring to a boil over medium-high heat, then drop the heat to low and gently simmer for 2½ hours. The ideal temperature to simmer a stock is around 205°F (96°C). Visually, there should be just a couple bubbles rising ever so gently.

5   Add the vegetables, the thyme, peppercorns, and bay leaf. Simmer for an additional 2½ hours.

6   Prepare an ice bath in a large bowl. Strain the stock through a fine-mesh strainer into another large bowl, then place that bowl in the ice bath to cool the liquid quickly. Discard the chicken parts and vegetables.

7   Transfer the stock to airtight containers and store in the fridge for up to 5 days or in the freezer for up to 3 months.

DARK CHICKEN STOCK

1 pound (454 grams) chicken feet

1 pound (454 grams) chicken backs

Neutral oil, such as sunflower, grapeseed, or vegetable

1 large yellow onion

2 large carrots

2 celery ribs

15 fresh thyme sprigs

10 black peppercorns

1 bay leaf (or 2 dried)

SPECIAL EQUIPMENT:

instant-read thermometer

When it comes to sauces, I much prefer the base richness that a dark stock provides. Unless I'm specifically going for something light and neutral, I reach for this stock most often.

1 Preheat the oven to 450°F (233°C). Fit a wire rack into a half sheet pan.

2 Pat the chicken feet and backs dry with paper towels, then place in a large bowl and lightly dress with some of the oil. Arrange the chicken on the rack. Place in the oven and roast for 20 to 25 minutes, or a deep brown. Transfer the chicken parts to a bowl or plate. Keep the rack and sheet pan handy. Keep the oven on.

3 Meanwhile, roughly chop the onion, carrots, and celery (the mirepoix) into similarly sized pieces (mirepoix cut). Place in a medium bowl and lightly dress with some of the oil. Arrange the vegetables on the rack and roast for 15 to 20 minutes, until gaining some color. Transfer to a plate or bowl.

4 Add the chicken parts to a stockpot and cover with water. Bring to a boil over high heat, then lower the heat to low and gently simmer for 2½ hours, occasionally skimming any foam that rises to the top of the pot. The ideal temperature to simmer a stock is around 205°F (96°C). Visually, there should be just a couple bubbles rising ever so gently.

5 Add the roasted vegetable mixture, the thyme, peppercorns, and bay leaf. Simmer for an additional 2½ hours.

6 Prepare an ice bath in a large bowl. Scoop out the chicken and vegetables, then strain the liquid through a fine-mesh strainer into another bowl, then place that bowl in the ice bath to cool the liquid quickly. Discard the chicken parts and vegetables.

7 Transfer the stock to airtight containers and store in the fridge for up to 5 days or in the freezer for up to 3 months.

DUCK JUS

5 medium shallots

1 bulb of garlic

2 pounds (907 grams) duck bones (from about 1 duck)

Neutral oil, such as sunflower, grapeseed, or vegetable

½ cup (4 fluid ounces; 125 milliliters) apple brandy

2 quarts (1.8 liters) Dark Chicken Stock (page 85)

10 fresh thyme sprigs

10 black peppercorns

1 fresh bay leaf (or 2 dried)

2 tablespoons cold unsalted butter

Kosher salt and freshly ground black pepper

Almost every restaurant I've worked in has had duck on the menu, and we never let any of it go to waste. The legs were cooked into duck confit, the breasts hung and aged to be pan-seared later, the skin rendered for cooking fat, and the bones used for stocks and sauces. A sauce that starts with duck bones is gamier, with a stronger poultry flavor, compared to a sauce that uses chicken stock as its base.

1   Preheat the oven to 450°F (233°C). Fit a wire rack into a half sheet pan.

2   Peel and slice the shallots into ¼-inch-thick rings. Cut off the root end from the garlic bulb, keeping the bulb intact. Then cut the bulb in half horizontally so you have 2 pieces, each held together by the garlic skins.

3   Arrange the duck bones on the rack and roast in the oven for 20 to 25 minutes, until bones are deep brown.

4   Heat a stockpot or small rondeau pan (or brazier) over medium heat. Add a small amount of oil to coat the bottom of the pot. When the oil starts to shimmer, add the garlic halves, cut side down, and toast until golden. Flip the garlic, then add the shallots and cook, stirring often, until translucent. Stir in the brandy to deglaze the pot, and then reduce about 4 minutes, until it's thick and *miroir* shiny (like a mirror).

5   Add the roasted duck bones, then the stock, thyme, peppercorns, and bay leaf. Bring to a simmer over medium-high heat and skim any foam and fat that rise to the surface. Scrape the sides of the pot with a rubber spatula periodically to incorporate the stuck bits back into the sauce. You want the flavor of the bits in the sauce, not on the side of the pot!

6   Continue to simmer until the sauce has started to thicken, about 45 minutes more.

7   Scoop out the solids, then strain the liquid through a fine-mesh strainer into a medium pot. (If you were to reduce the liquid all the way, with all the bones and vegetables in there, some of the sauce will cling to the solids, reducing the yield.) Continue to reduce the liquid for 30 to 45 minutes more, skimming any foam or fat on the surface and scraping the sides of the pot, until the sauce is *nappe* (coats the back of a spoon).

8   Turn off the heat and whisk in the cold butter. Adjust the seasoning with salt and black pepper.

9   Serve immediately. Alternatively, pour the sauce into a small bowl and place the bowl in an ice bath to cool quickly, then transfer to an airtight container. Store in the fridge for up to 5 days or freezer for up to 3 months.

BEEF AND MUSHROOM REDUCTION

2 quarts (1.8 liters) Beef Stock (page 82)

5 small shallots

3 garlic cloves

3 tablespoons neutral oil, such as sunflower, grapeseed, or vegetable

1½ cups (354 milliliters) Mushroom Stock (page 88)

5 fresh thyme sprigs

5 black peppercorns

1 fresh bay leaf (or 2 dried)

1 tablespoon cold unsalted butter

Kosher salt and freshly ground black pepper

This reduction is similar to Bordelaise (page 90), but instead of wine, it uses mushroom stock. The earthiness of the mushrooms complements the richness of the beef stock, and this harmonious combination is a lovely match for grilled meat. Think Rib Steak and Grilled Mushrooms (page 185).

1 Warm the beef stock in a large saucepan over medium-low heat and keep warm. Have a rubber spatula or pastry brush nearby to clean the sides of the pot. If necessary, occasionally skim the foam from the surface of the stock.

2 Slice the shallots ¼ inch thick. Smash the garlic.

3 Heat the oil in a medium saucepan over medium heat. When it is shimmering, add the garlic and brown on all sides, about 3 minutes. Add the shallots and cook, stirring often, until translucent, about 3 minutes. Add the mushroom stock and bring to a boil over medium-high heat. Reduce until you have about ½ cup, about 12 minutes. The flavor should be strong to stand up to the beef stock.

4 Add half the beef stock, the thyme, peppercorns, and bay leaf. Continue to cook about 20 minutes, until it has reduced by about half and starts to thicken. Use the spatula to clean the sides of the pot to loosen any sticky stuff and stir it into the liquid. Also, occasionally skim the surface to remove any foam.

5 Add the remaining beef stock and cook about 20 minutes to reduce the liquid again by about half. When it starts to thicken again, strain the liquid into a small or medium saucepan. (As it thickens up, the liquid will cling to the shallots and aromatics and yield a bit less sauce.)

6 Continue reducing the sauce until *nappe* (coats the back of a spoon), 30 to 40 minutes more. To check the consistency, pour a small amount onto a plate. It shouldn't be watery and should hold its shape. When you're happy with the consistency, reduce the heat to the lowest setting and whisk in the cold butter. Adjust the seasoning with salt and pepper.

7 Keep the sauce warm until ready to serve. Alternatively, pour the sauce into a small bowl and set in an ice bath to cool quickly, then transfer to an airtight container. Refrigerate for up to 5 days or freeze for 3 months.

MUSHROOM STOCK

2 pounds (907 grams) fresh cremini mushrooms

5 small shallots

1 bulb of garlic

¼ cup (59 milliliters) extra-virgin olive oil

3 quarts (2.8 liters) water

15 fresh thyme sprigs

10 black peppercorns

1 fresh bay leaf (or 2 dried)

Mushroom stock is a cooking ingredient everyone should have in their repertoire. It offers a big blast of umami flavor and is great for vegetarian dishes, like my Tagliatelle and Morels (page 163).

1   Clean the cremini mushrooms with a damp cloth. Alternatively, give them a quick dunk in water, then wipe with a dry cloth. Slice the mushrooms and shallots into ¼-inch-thick pieces.

2   Cut off the root end from the bulb of garlic, keeping the bulb intact. Then cut the bulb in half horizontally so you have 2 pieces, each held together by the skins.

3   Heat a stockpot over medium-high heat and add the olive oil. When the oil starts to shimmer, add the mushrooms. It will seem like a lot, but they will release a lot of water and shrink. Cook about 15 minutes, stirring frequently, until there is no more water and the mushrooms start to turn golden.

4   Nestle the garlic halves, cut side down, into the bottom of the pot and toast about 2 minutes, until golden. Flip them over and stir in the shallots. Cook about 4 minutes, stirring occasionally, until the shallots are translucent. Deglaze the pot with the water, using a rubber spatula to loosen all the stuck bits (*fond*) on the bottom of the pot.

5   Add the thyme, peppercorns, and bay leaf to the stockpot. Bring to a boil over high heat, then reduce the heat to low and simmer gently for 1 hour.

6   Turn off the heat and cover the pot with its lid. Let steep for an additional 1 hour.

7   Prepare an ice bath in a large bowl. Strain the cooking liquid through a fine-mesh strainer into a medium bowl, pressing on the mushrooms to squeeze out all the liquid. Place that bowl in the ice bath to cool the liquid quickly.

8   Transfer the stock to airtight containers. Refrigerate for up to 1 week or freeze for 3 months.

CHARRED ONION BROTH

8 large yellow onions

4 quarts (3.8 liters) water

SPECIAL EQUIPMENT:

instant-read
thermometer

Many people associate bitterness with a bad taste, and sometimes that's true. But most of the time we add bitterness to a dish and nobody has a clue. That's because it's an important balancing tool for sweetness. Case in point: this broth, which comes from my time spent at the restaurant Auburn. Onions are high in sugar (think about how sweet slow-cooked caramelized onions get), and by adding some bitterness in the form of char, you make a delicious balanced broth with only one primary ingredient. Use this to make the Charred Onion Vinaigrette (page 73).

1   Preheat the oven to 350°F (177°C). Fit a wire rack in a half sheet pan.

2   Cut off the top and bottom of each onion, then remove the skin and first layer. Lay the onion trimmings on the rack and place in the oven to roast for 20 to 40 minutes, or until deep brown overall and black in some spots.

3   Meanwhile, roughly slice the remaining whole onions. Place the onions and the charred onion bits in a stockpot and add the water. Cover with the lid and heat on the lowest setting you can. Ideally, you want to keep the liquid at around 200°F (93°C), which is just below a simmer. You want as little evaporation as possible for this broth. Simmer for 6 hours.

4   Strain the liquid through a sieve into a large pot. You should have about 3½ quarts. Place the pot over low heat and reduce the liquid until it is much darker in color and no longer tastes watery; at this point there should be about 1 quart of liquid.

5   Prepare an ice bath in a large bowl. Transfer the broth to a large glass jar or medium bowl and place in the ice bath to cool quickly.

6   Store the broth in the fridge for up to 5 days or in the freezer for 3 months.

BORDELAISE

FOR THE RED WINE REDUCTION

5 small shallots

3 garlic cloves

3 cups (675 milliliters) dry red wine

10 black peppercorns

5 fresh thyme sprigs

1 fresh bay leaf (or 2 dried)

FOR THE BEEF REDUCTION

2 quarts (1.8 liters) Beef Stock (page 82)

5 small shallots

3 garlic cloves

3 tablespoons neutral oil, such as sunflower, grapeseed, or vegetable

8 ounces (226 grams) beef bones, neck, and knuckle

3 tablespoons cold unsalted butter

5 fresh thyme sprigs

1 fresh bay leaf (or 2 dried)

Kosher salt and freshly ground black pepper

Bordelaise is a classic French sauce named for the Bordeaux region in France. It's wine heavy, beefy, and old-school French cooking. Many recipes call for dumping wine and beef stock in a pot, reducing the hell out of it, and calling it a day. We can do so much better. This recipe builds flavors each step of the way, infusing and reducing the wine separately, using bones with marrow (a classic but often overlooked step in traditional bordelaise), and throwing in lots of aromatics. The result is intensely flavorful and complex.

MAKE THE RED WINE REDUCTION

1 Peel the shallots and smash the garlic, then add to a medium saucepan. Add the wine, peppercorns, thyme, and bay leaf.

2 Bring to a boil over medium-high heat, then reduce the heat to medium low and simmer. About 45 minutes, until reduced to 1 cup.

MAKE THE BEEF REDUCTION

1 Place the beef stock in a large saucepan over medium-low heat.

2 Slice the shallots and garlic ¼ inch thick.

3 Heat the oil in a large sauté pan (or shallow straight-sided pan) or saucepan over medium heat. When the oil is shimmering and begins to smoke, add the beef bones and brown on all sides, about 2 minutes per side. Add the shallots and cook, tossing occasionally, for 2 minutes. Add the garlic and cook 3 to 4 minutes, tossing occasionally, until the shallots are translucent and the garlic is toasted and starting to brown.

4 Add 2 tablespoons of the butter and swirl the pan until it browns. Deglaze the pot with ¾ cup of the red wine reduction. Scrape the bottom and sides of the pot to release any built-up fond. (Save the remaining red wine reduction for later adjustments, if necessary; that's a good trick I've used as a saucier.)

5 Add 1 quart of the warm stock, the thyme, and bay leaf to the sauté pan and bring to a simmer. Continue to simmer for about 30 minutes, until the liquid begins to thicken and have a little body. Have a rubber spatula or a pastry brush nearby to dip in water and clean the sides of the pan to incorporate that sticky stuff into the sauce—it adds flavor and prevents burning. Occasionally, skim any foam that rises to the top. (To make this skimming easier, you can place your pan slightly off center; the bubbles will push the fat to one side of the pan, saving you a bit of time.)

6 Add the remaining quart of stock and continue reducing the liquid. When the sauce begins to thicken up and gain body again, in approximately 30 minutes, strain the liquid into a medium saucepan.

7 Continue reducing the sauce until it's *nappe* (coats the back of a spoon). To check the consistency, pour a small amount onto a plate. It should hold its shape and not appear watery. When you're happy with the consistency, reduce the heat to the lowest setting and whisk in the remaining tablespoon of cold butter. Adjust the seasoning to taste with salt and pepper. If you want the sauce more acidic, add some of the remaining red wine reduction.

FINISH AND SERVE

1 Keep the sauce warm until ready to serve. Alternatively, pour the sauce into a small bowl and place in an ice bath to cool it quickly, then transfer it to an airtight container.

2 Refrigerate for up to 5 days or freeze for 3 months.

STARTERS

BITES THAT SET THE STAGE. PUFFED, BLISTERED, ROASTED; SPICY, CREAMY, HERBAL; FUNKY, FRESH, SMOKY—IT'S ALL HERE.

Serves 4

PUFFED BEEF TENDON

1 pound (454 grams) boneless beef tendon

2 cups (118 milliliters) neutral oil, such as sunflower, grapeseed, or vegetable, or beef tallow

Hot Sauce Powder (page 40) or Salt and Vinegar Powder (page 39), for serving

SPECIAL EQUIPMENT:

electric pressure cooker, deli slicer (optional), dehydrator (optional), instant-read thermometer

Presenting off-cuts (aka inexpensive, less popular cuts of meat) in exciting ways is always on my mind. There's a fairly prominent taboo against off-cuts and offal in the United States. If you go to a chain grocery store, you'll be hard-pressed to find any of these cuts. But that's not the case elsewhere in the world. And one thing I've noticed when I'm cooking is that if it at least looks familiar, people are more open to it, such as this beef tendon, which puffs up like a chicharron when deep-fried.

PRESSURE-COOK THE TENDON

1   Place the beef tendon in the pressure cooker and add just enough water to cover. Secure the lid and cook on high pressure for 1 hour, then follow natural release method before opening.

2   Lay the tendon in a quarter sheet pan. Pat dry with paper towels. Place another quarter sheet pan on top of the tendon, then set some heavy items on top. Let this weight press the meat overnight in the fridge (see Note).

DEHYDRATE THE TENDON

1   If you have a deli slicer, use it to slice the tendon into pieces about ⅛ inch thick. If not, use a very sharp knife to slice as thin as possible. (To do this, use the full length of your knife to make long slices into the tendon. If you need to slice more than once to get a clean cut, that's totally fine.) As long as all the tendon pieces are about the same thickness, they'll dehydrate at the same rate. You can also opt for slightly thicker slices, which would yield a thicker puff. I prefer them very thin.

2   *Option 1:* Lay the thin strips of tendon on a dehydrator tray and dry at 160°F (71°C) for 3 hours, until completely crisp.

Option 2: Preheat the oven to 170°F (76°C). Place a wire rack in a quarter sheet pan and lay the strips on the rack. Roast in the oven until completely crisp and dry, about 2½ hours, keeping a careful eye on the meat.

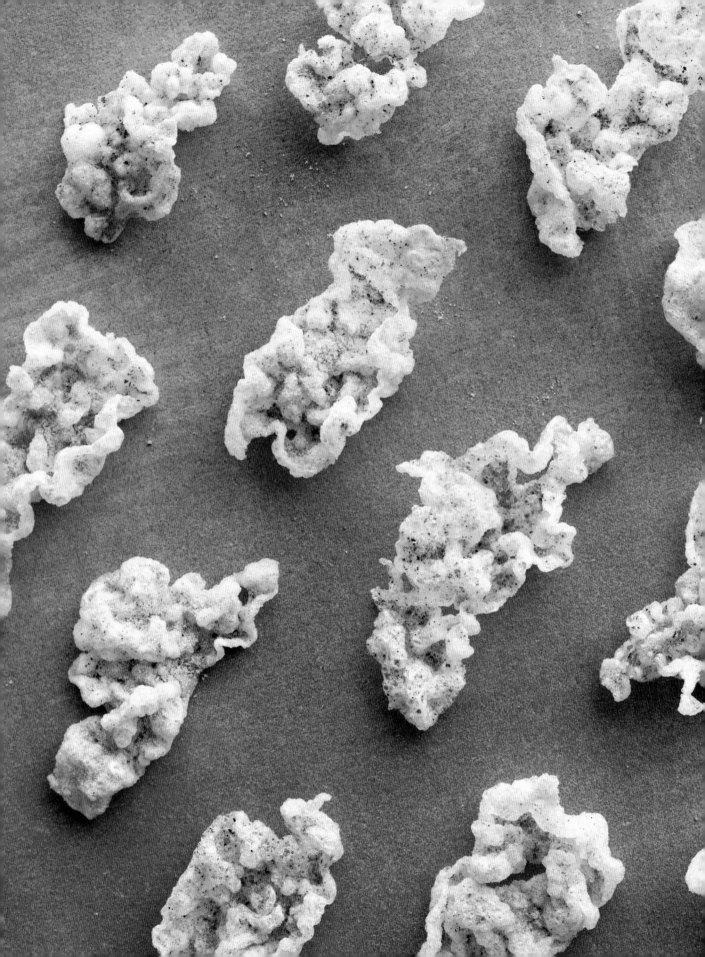

FRY THE TENDON AND SERVE

1 Heat the oil in a deep-fryer or tall-sided pot to 350°F (177°C). (Bonus points if you use beef tallow!) Working in batches, drop in the tendon pieces and fry until they puff up, less than 30 seconds each. Place on a paper towel–lined plate to drain while you finish the frying.

2 To serve, dust the strips with either Hot Sauce Powder or Salt and Vinegar Powder. These are best eaten the day they are fried.

NOTE

After the beef tendon has been pressed, you can freeze it. Thaw it overnight in the fridge, then proceed with the frying. But if you do have a deli slicer, skip the thawing and leave the meat frozen—it's easier to slice this way.

OYSTERS, COCONUT, AND CUCUMBER
WITH CILANTRO-SERRANO OIL

FOR THE CILANTRO-SERRANO OIL

1 bunch fresh cilantro

2 fresh serrano chiles, stems removed

½ cup (118 milliliters) sunflower oil

FOR THE OYSTERS AND TOPPINGS

3 ounces (80 grams) cucumber

1 finger lime (see Notes)

¼ cup (59 milliliters) coconut cream

2 teaspoons fish sauce

6 oysters (your favorite kind)

SPECIAL EQUIPMENT:

high-powered blender, oyster knife

An oyster purist will say you shouldn't eat oysters with anything at all. And to them I say "Boring!" Oysters are so much fun to play around with.

You'll almost always see oysters served in restaurants with a mignonette and/or hot sauce, but these oysters go heavy on the Southeast Asian flavors. They're served with cilantro, chiles, coconut cream, and finger limes, the latter of which add a burst of acid that plays well with the saltiness of the oysters and provides a really pleasant texture.

MAKE THE CILANTRO-SERRANO OIL

1 Bring a medium saucepan of water to a boil over high heat. Meanwhile, prepare an ice bath in a large bowl.

2 Drop the cilantro into the boiling water, stems and all, and blanch for 15 seconds. Quickly remove the cilantro from the water and dunk into the ice bath. Lift the cilantro up and squeeze out as much water as you can, then lay it on a tray or plate to dry.

3 Cut the serrano chiles in half. Place in a small saucepan (seeds and all), and add the sunflower oil. Place the saucepan over medium heat and gently fry for about 5 minutes, until the chiles are blistered all over and soft. Turn off the heat and let the chiles cool completely.

4 Add the chiles and oil to the blender, then add the cilantro. Blend on high until the oil is bright green, about 3 minutes. Strain the paste through a fine-mesh strainer lined with cheesecloth or a coffee filter. Transfer to an airtight container and store in the fridge until ready to use.

PREPARE THE TOPPINGS

1 Peel and seed the cucumber. Julienne and then finely dice the cucumber (*brunoise*). Place in a small bowl, cover, and store in the fridge until ready to use.

2 Cut open the finger lime on one end and pinch from the opposite end to push out all the lime caviar.

3 Add the coconut cream and fish sauce to a small bowl and whisk to blend well. Cover and store in the fridge until ready to use. (It's best to use this the same day as made.)

PREPARE THE OYSTERS AND SERVE

1 Use an oyster knife to find the hinge in each oyster and insert the tip of the knife until secure. Give it a little wiggle—it should feel snug inside the hinge. Carefully twist the knife and pop open the oyster (see Note). Turn the knife and angle it upward to slide underneath the top shell and release the oyster. Discard the top shell. Use your finger or a towel to wipe around the lip of the oyster to clean away any gunk. Take the knife and slide it underneath the oyster to free it from the bottom shell, and optionally flip the oyster. Place 2 oysters each on 3 serving plates.

2 To each oyster, add a few drops of the coconut cream–fish sauce and then the cilantro-serrano oil. Place some cucumber dice and some finger-lime caviar on top and serve immediately.

NOTES

When cut open, finger limes reveal a filling of tiny lime caviar filled with tart citrusy juice. They're grown in California and Florida, and they can sometimes be found at specialty food stores or farmers' markets. If you can't find them, finish with a squeeze of lime instead.

Opening oysters is more about leverage than about brute force. If you're pushing rather than twisting, you might stab the oyster or, worse, your hand could slip and you could hurt yourself.

HIRAMASA AGUACHILE

½ large (about 5 ounces) garden cucumber

2 fresh jalapeños

2 fresh serrano chiles

2 garlic cloves

½ bunch fresh cilantro, plus more for garnish

4 tablespoons fresh lime juice, plus more for dressing

Kosher salt

¼ small red onion

1 small Persian cucumber

3 small radishes

Extra-virgin olive oil

6 ounces (170 grams) hiramasa (amberjack) or hamachi (yellowtail), or any sushi-grade fish you like

Flaky sea salt, such as Maldon

Cilantro-Serrano Oil (from recipe on page 100)

SPECIAL EQUIPMENT:

high-powered blender

Aguachile is similar to Peruvian ceviche, the primary differences being the marinade and the provenance. Aguachile is from Mexico. Having grown up in Los Angeles, I'm used to seeing it everywhere; some version of it can be found on the menus of a lot of restaurants. And on any given lunch break, it's standard to go outside and buy some aguachile from a street vendor, who serves it with tortilla chips. My version uses raw fish instead of the classic shrimp.

1   Peel the cucumber. Split the jalapeños and serrano chiles open and remove the seeds.

2   Place the cucumber, jalapeños, serrano chiles, and garlic in the blender. Add the cilantro, 2 tablespoons of the lime juice, and a pinch of salt. Blend until completely smooth, then pass through a fine-mesh strainer lined with cheesecloth. You can ball up and squeeze the cheesecloth slightly, but be careful not to push out any sediment. It's best to let the cheesecloth hang, draining naturally in the fridge for an hour. Cover and keep chilled until ready to serve. (This aguachile broth should be made the day you plan to use it, as it will brown and oxidize rapidly.)

3   Prepare an ice bath in a large bowl. Thinly slice the red onion, about ¼ inch thick, then place the onion in the ice bath for 3 minutes. This will crisp it up and get rid of that really harsh raw onion bite. Drain.

4   Thinly slice the Persian cucumber and radish into ¼-inch-thick rounds. Add both to a small bowl, season with a pinch of salt, and dress with olive oil and the remaining 2 tablespoons lime juice.

5   Cut the fish into ⅜-inch-thick slices. (Don't slice too thin or it'll just disappear and lose texture.)

6   Season each slice of fish with a small pinch of flaky salt and arrange in 4 serving bowls. Add 3 to 4 pieces each of the dressed cucumber and radishes on top. Place the red onion slices on top of that, then garnish with the cilantro leaves.

7   Lastly, check and, if desired, season the aguachile with salt. Pour in the broth until it comes just under the top of the fish. Finish with a drizzle of the cilantro-serrano oil and serve immediately.

GRILLED PRAWNS
WITH SALSA MACHA

3 dried guajillo chiles

2 dried ancho chiles

3 dried Morita chiles

3 dried chiles de arbol

4 garlic cloves

½ cup (75 grams) unsalted raw peanuts

¼ cup white sesame seeds

1 cup (250 milliliters) sunflower oil

1 tablespoon dried Mexican oregano

Kosher salt

2 teaspoons sherry vinegar

1 pound (454 grams) New Caledonian prawns, or any large shrimp, preferably not shelled and deveined

1 medium lime

SPECIAL EQUIPMENT:

high-powered blender

Originating in Veracruz, Mexico, salsa macha is an incredibly flavorful chile oil made with dried chiles, toasted nuts, and seeds. And it's one of my all-time favorite condiments. Even if you don't make the prawns, make the salsa macha—and put it on everything.

MAKE THE SALSA MACHA

1   Cut open the guajillo, ancho, and Morita chiles. Remove the stems, seeds, and ribs. Place in a heat-safe bowl and add the whole chiles de arbol.

2   Thinly slice the garlic and add to a small saucepan. Add the peanuts, sesame seeds, and sunflower oil, then place the pan over medium-low heat and cook gently for 5 to 7 minutes, until the peanuts, sesame seeds, and garlic start to turn golden brown.

3   Pour the hot oil mixture over the dried chiles. Let sit for 5 minutes, then add the Mexican oregano. Let sit for another 30 minutes to allow the chiles to hydrate and soften up.

4   Transfer the chile mixture to the blender. Add a pinch of salt. Blend on low, scraping down the sides as needed, until everything is about the same size but still fairly chunky. Add the vinegar and taste, adding more salt, if needed. Transfer the salsa macha to a container and store in the fridge if you're not using it right away.

COOK THE PRAWNS AND SERVE

1   Heat a grill until very hot.

2   If the prawns are not cleaned, remove the shells around the body but leave on the heads if possible, as well as the tails. Using a toothpick, tweezers, or small fish pliers, stick your tool right behind the head, on the back, to get underneath the vein. Pull up to expose the vein, then pull it out. It should come out in one piece and make the tail jump a little. (I like this method because you don't need to cut open the prawns to devein them, and they look a little nicer. If you're having trouble getting out the vein this way, use your knife to make a shallow cut along the back of the body where the vein is and pull it out.)

3   Season both sides of the prawns with salt and place on the grill. Let them cook mostly on one side for about 2 minutes to get a nice char, then flip them and cook for about 30 seconds more to finish the cooking. (You can also sauté the prawns in a large skillet over medium-high heat.) You'll know the prawns are done when they curl into a nice C shape and are a vibrant pink. When they start curling tighter, that's an indicator that they're overdone and rubbery, so be sure to remove them from the grill before that happens.

4   Place the prawns on serving plates. Hit them with a big squeeze of lime juice and top with a generous spoonful of the salsa macha. Serve immediately.

NOTE

Just about everything tastes good with salsa macha. I also love to slather it over corn on the cob. Brush cooked corn cobs with the salsa macha oil, quarter the cobs into smaller pieces, then top with salsa macha crunchy bits and Cotija cheese.

SNAP PEAS
WITH CALIFORNIA KOSHO AND MINT

1 pound (454 grams) sugar snap peas

1 tablespoon California Kosho (page 48)

1 teaspoon extra-virgin olive oil, plus more as needed

¼ cup (59 milliliters) fresh mint leaves

1 tablespoon fresh lemon juice

1 handful pea shoots

Lemon-infused olive oil

Kosher salt

This dish combines something old with something very new: salty preserved California kosho from last summer and super-fresh and bright snap peas and pea shoots from this spring.

1   To remove any tough strings from the sugar snap peas, use a small knife to make a cut through the stem end of the pea, stopping just before you go all the way through. Pull slightly at an angle away from the pea, following the concave side, and the long fibrous strand will come away—kind of like opening a zipper. (This is an optional step, but it makes eating them a nicer experience, since nothing will get stuck in your teeth.)

2   Place the kosho and 1 teaspoon olive oil in a small bowl and stir to combine.

3   Heat a large sauté pan (or shallow straight-sided pan) over medium-high heat and add a few tablespoons of olive oil. Add the peas and let them blister on one side, about 2 minutes. Toss them in the pan and blister the other side, about 2 minutes more.

4   Turn the heat off and add the kosho mixture. Toss to coat well, then add the mint. Toss once or twice, until the mint wilts. Transfer the seasoned peas to a serving bowl.

5   Place the pea shoots in a small bowl and lightly dress with the lemon-flavored olive oil. Season with some salt, then scatter the shoots on top of the snap peas in the bowl. Serve immediately.

SUMMER SQUASH
WITH GREEN CURRY AND LIME LEAF PEANUTS

3 lemongrass stalks

5 fresh serrano chiles

1 2-inch knob fresh ginger

1 small shallot

3 garlic cloves

1 tablespoon fish sauce, or more as desired

1 teaspoon ground coriander

Neutral oil, such as sunflower, grapeseed, or vegetable

1 13-ounce can coconut cream

1 lime

1 cup (15 grams) fresh cilantro leaves, plus more for serving

Kosher salt

4 medium zucchini or summer squash

Lime Leaf Peanuts (page 26)

SPECIAL EQUIPMENT:

high-powered blender, Microplane or other grater

Grilled summer squash gets the deluxe treatment with this spicy and fragrant green curry sauce. Crushed, roasted peanuts would do as a garnish, but the Lime Leaf Peanuts (page 26) are really the way to go. If those aren't in your pantry yet, now is the time to change that.

MAKE THE GREEN CURRY SAUCE

1   Remove the tough outer leaves from the lemongrass stalks. Slice off the lower bulb and the upper portion of the stalk where it is mostly green and woody and discard. Thinly slice the bottom stem parts and add to the blender.

2   Remove the stem and seeds from the serrano chiles. Peel and thinly slice the ginger. Add to the blender. Roughly chop the shallot and add to the blender along with the garlic.

3   Add the tablespoon of fish sauce and the ground coriander to the blender. Blend as smooth as you can, scraping down the sides frequently.

4   Heat a few tablespoons of the oil in a large sauté pan (or shallow straight-sided pan) over medium-high heat. When the oil begins to smoke, add the curry paste and fry for 3 to 4 minutes, stirring constantly, until extremely fragrant.

5   Reduce the heat to medium-low, add the coconut cream, and bring to a simmer. Simmer for 30 minutes, stirring occasionally.

6   Meanwhile, use the Microplane to zest the lime, then juice the lime.

7   Strain the curry sauce through a fine-mesh strainer into the blender, pressing down with a rubber spatula to push through as much liquid as possible.

8   Add the cup of cilantro leaves, the lime zest, and lime juice to the blender. Blend until the mixture is bright green. Taste and adjust the seasoning with salt and/or more fish sauce.

COOK THE SQUASH AND SERVE

1 Heat a grill until hot. Slice the squash lengthwise into ½-inch-thick planks. Lightly brush the planks with some of the oil and season with some salt. Place on the grill and grill until just tender, 2 to 3 minutes per side. (Alternatively, you can sauté the squash in a large skillet on the stovetop, 2 to 3 minutes per side, until lightly charred.)

2 Divide the squash among 4 serving bowls and pour in the curry sauce around the squash. Top each serving with some of the peanuts and some cilantro leaves.

SHISHITOS
WITH BONITO AIOLI AND PUFFED GRAINS

1¼ cups (295 milliliters) sunflower oil, plus more for cooking

1½ cups (15 grams) bonito flakes

1 lemon

3 garlic cloves

1½-inch knob fresh ginger

3 large egg yolks

1 tablespoon soy sauce

Kosher salt

1 lime

1 tablespoon fish sauce

8 ounces (227 grams) shishito peppers

¼ cup (about 15 grams) Puffed Grains (page 43)

SPECIAL EQUIPMENT:

high-powered blender, Microplane or other zester

Shishito peppers topped with wiggling bonito flakes are iconic, and this is just a riff on that. I love to eat shishitos with a dipping sauce alongside, so that's where the bonito aioli comes in.

MAKE THE BONITO AIOLI

1 Combine the 1¼ cups sunflower oil and the bonito flakes in a medium saucepan and place over medium-low heat. Cook about 5 minutes, until the bonito flakes turn somewhat translucent and there are small bubbles rising. Turn off the heat and let cool to room temperature while steeping. Use a cheesecloth-lined strainer to separate the bonito flakes from the oil, pressing out as much oil as you can.

2 Use the Microplane to zest the lemon, then squeeze the lemon until you have about 3 tablespoons of juice. Grate the garlic and ginger with the Microplane.

3 To the blender, add the bonito flakes, the egg yolks, 2 tablespoons of the lemon juice (save the remaining tablespoon for the shishitos), the lemon zest, the garlic, ginger, and soy sauce. Blend until it's fairly smooth.

4 Slowly stream in the bonito oil, scraping down the sides of the blender with a rubber spatula as needed. Taste the aioli and adjust the seasoning with salt, if needed. If not using right away, transfer to an airtight container and store in the fridge for up to 5 days.

COOK THE SHISHITOS AND SERVE

1 Juice the lime and add 1 tablespoon of the juice to a small bowl. Add the fish sauce and the remaining tablespoon lemon juice and whisk to combine.

2 Heat a large sauté pan over medium heat and add just enough oil to coat the bottom. When the oil starts to smoke, add the shishitos and a small pinch of salt. Let cook for 3 minutes, until the shishitos are nicely blistered. Flip the shishitos and blister the other side, another 2 minutes.

3 Deglaze the pan with the lime-fish sauce mixture and reduce the liquid for about 2 minutes, until it's thick and tacky and coats the shishitos nicely.

4 Add a spoonful of aioli to one side of a serving plate and arrange the shishitos on the other side. Sprinkle with the puffed grains and serve.

BRUSSELS SPROUTS
WITH CHORIZO BREAD CRUMBS

4 cups (150 grams) day-old country or sourdough bread cubes

3½ ounces (100 grams) Spanish dry-cured chorizo sausage

1 tablespoon fresh rosemary leaves

Kosher salt

1 pound (454 grams) Brussels sprouts

3 tablespoons neutral oil, such as sunflower, grapeseed, or vegetable

1 tablespoon sherry vinegar

SPECIAL EQUIPMENT:

food processor

Brussels sprouts can be hit or miss—probably because a lot of people have bad associations from their childhood memories. But here's a fun fact: in the last couple of decades, farmers have been selectively breeding Brussels sprouts to be much less bitter. So, if you think you don't like sprouts but it's been a while since you've had any, try them now. These are covered in chorizo bread crumbs, a nod to the vegetable's classic bacon pairing, but a little more refined.

MAKE THE CHORIZO BREAD CRUMBS

1   Preheat the oven to 350°F (177°C).

2   Spread the bread cubes on a half sheet pan and bake about 20 minutes, until completely dried out and golden brown. Let cool completely. Keep the oven on.

3   Remove the casing from the chorizo and slice into ¼-inch rounds. Spread the rounds on a quarter sheet pan and roast in the oven for 15 minutes, until the chorizo starts to crisp on the outside and a good amount of fat has rendered out. Transfer the chorizo to a paper towel–lined plate to absorb any excess fat. Let cool completely.

4   Meanwhile, roughly chop the rosemary and transfer to the food processer. Add the chorizo and pulse until the chorizo is crumbly. Add the bread cubes and a pinch of salt, then pulse again until everything is the same size. Transfer the crumbs to an airtight container until ready to use (use within 5 days).

ROAST THE BRUSSELS SPROUTS AND SERVE

1 Preheat the oven to 425°F (218°C).

2 Cut off a small section of the root end of each sprout, then cut the sprout in half.

3 Heat a large oven-safe sauté pan over medium-high heat and add a few tablespoons of oil. When the oil starts to smoke, add the Brussels sprouts cut side down and season with a pinch of salt. Cook 3 to 5 minutes, until the sprouts are a deep brown on the cut side, then give them a flip and transfer the pan to the oven. Roast for 10 to 12 minutes, until the Brussels sprouts are tender.

4 Deglaze the pan with the sherry vinegar. Taste a Brussels sprout and adjust seasoning with salt, if needed. Add a pinch of the chorizo bread crumbs to the mixture and toss.

5 Place the Brussels sprouts in a large serving bowl and top with generous handfuls of the bread crumbs, then serve.

NOTES

Leftover chorizo bread crumbs taste amazing when sprinkled over eggs and pasta.

Let's talk about sherry vinegar. In my opinion, it should replace the bottle of balsamic in your cupboard. You need to pay a pretty penny for a good balsamic vinegar, and the cheap stuff you'll find in the store is usually loaded with sweeteners. You can, on the other hand, get good sherry vinegar on a budget. It's bright and complex with caramel notes and a touch of nuttiness.

ROASTED BABY CARROTS
WITH SPICED LABNE AND PISTACHIO DUKKAH

2 pounds (907 grams) baby carrots

1 pound (453 grams) labne (see Note)

3 garlic cloves

1 lemon

1 tablespoon Aleppo pepper

1 tablespoon ground sumac

1 teaspoon ground cumin

1 tablespoon ground coriander

Kosher salt

1 1-inch knob fresh ginger

3 tablespoons extra-virgin olive oil

¼ cup (40 grams) Pistachio Dukkah (page 32)

Fresh cilantro leaves, for garnish

SPECIAL EQUIPMENT:

Microplane or other grater

In my restaurant experience, I've found that carrots are most often used in a mirepoix or in soups. But roasted carrots are so good that they deserve to be their own dish.

1   Preheat the oven to 425°F (218°C).

2   If your carrots are pretty clean, scrub them with a vegetable brush and dry well. If they're dirty, peel them.

3   Place the labne in a medium bowl. Using the Microplane, grate the garlic and zest of the lemon into the bowl. Cut the lemon in half and squeeze one half, then add the juice. Add the Aleppo pepper, sumac, cumin, and coriander. Add a pinch of salt and stir to combine. Taste and adjust the seasoning as needed.

4   Peel the ginger. Cut out a small square of cheesecloth and grate the ginger onto the cheesecloth. Wrap it up like a little package and tie with kitchen twine.

5   Heat the olive oil in a large oven-safe sauté pan over medium heat. When the oil begins to shimmer and barely smoke, add the carrots in a single layer. Add a pinch of salt and sear the carrots about 3 minutes, until you get a nice color on one side. Flip the carrots and place them in the oven to roast for 8 minutes, until tender. (Alternatively, you can cook the carrots completely in the oven. Dress them with oil and salt, place them in a preheated half sheet pan, and roast for 10 to 15 minutes, stirring halfway through, until tender.) Squeeze the packet of grated ginger over the warm carrots.

6   Spoon a dollop of the spiced labne onto 4 serving plates and arrange some of the carrots on top. Sprinkle with the pistachio dukkah and garnish with the cilantro.

NOTE

Popular in Middle Eastern cuisine, labne is a thick and creamy strained yogurt.

COUNTRY LOAVES
WITH LEEK AND HERB BUTTER

2½ cups (600 milliliters) water

1 packet (7 grams) active dry yeast

4¾ cups (600 grams) all-purpose flour, plus more for surface

2½ cups (400 grams) semolina flour

¾ cup (80 milliliters) barley malt syrup

1 tablespoon kosher salt

Rice flour, for dusting (optional)

SPECIAL EQUIPMENT:

instant-read thermometer, stand mixer with dough hook

I'm a firm believer in having a personal loaf of bread with your meal. This little round is made with semolina, which gives it a wonderfully slightly dense texture. Serve this with Leek and Herb Butter (recipe follows).

1   Pour the water into a small saucepan and place over medium-low heat. Warm the water to 110°F (43°C).

2   Pour the warm water into the bowl of a stand mixer fitted with the hook attachment. Sprinkle the yeast over the top and let sit for 10 minutes. The water should turn slightly foamy.

3   To the bowl, add the all-purpose flour, the semolina flour, the barley malt syrup, and the salt. Mix on speed 2 (medium-low) for 8 minutes, until the dough is soft and supple. It may be a little tacky, but it shouldn't be sticky. If your mixer feels a bit small for this task, proceed to the next step.

4   Lightly flour a work surface and turn out the dough. If needed, continue to knead the dough, using your hands to push and press, until it's no longer sticky.

5   Portion the dough into 6 7-ounce pieces, then shape each piece into a ball.

6   Arrange the balls in a half sheet pan and cover with a clean kitchen towel. Proof until the dough balls have doubled in size, about 45 minutes. Optionally, dust the loaves with the rice flour and score the tops when they have risen.

7   Preheat the oven to 425°F (218°C). Arrange a rack in the center of the oven and add a pan to the bottom rack.

8   Place the loaves in the oven, and add a few ice cubes to the pan on the bottom rack. Bake the loaves for 20 minutes, or until the internal temperature of each is 190°F (87°C).

9   Serve the loaves on the same day as made. (Alternatively, you can tightly wrap the individual loaves with plastic and store in the freezer for up to 3 months.)

LEEK AND HERB BUTTER

1 bunch fresh chives, trimmed and cut into matchstick lengths

Leaves of 1 bunch fresh parsley

1½ cups (3 sticks; 340 grams) unsalted butter, ½ cup (1 stick; 113 grams) softened (see Note)

2 large leeks, white and pale green parts only

1 teaspoon kosher salt

Coarsely ground black pepper

Flaky sea salt, such as Maldon

SPECIAL EQUIPMENT:

high-powered blender

For an impressive and spreadable compound butter, cook a couple of leeks low and slow to draw out their sweetness, then blend with a ton of herbs and super-soft butter. To do it justice, serve the butter with the fresh-from-the-oven Country Loaves (preceding recipe). A bagel with lox is another solid vehicle.

1 Bring a large saucepan of water to a boil. Prepare an ice bath in a large bowl.

2 Add the chives and parsley to the boiling water and blanch for 15 seconds, stirring constantly. Strain through a fine-mesh strainer and add the herbs to the ice bath to cool. Lift and squeeze out as much water as possible, then spread the herbs out on a plate or tray to dry.

3 Add 1 cup (2 sticks) of the butter to a medium saucepan and melt over low heat.

4 Cut each leek in half lengthwise, then thinly slice. Add the leeks to the melted butter and simmer over very low heat (you want no color, no browning), stirring every few minutes until the leeks are tender and translucent, at least 30 minutes. Let cool to room temperature.

5 Place the leeks, including the butter, in the blender. Add the blanched herbs and the salt and blend until smooth. Pass the mixture through a tamis or fine-mesh strainer into a medium bowl.

6 Add the ½ cup softened butter to the herb-butter mixture in the bowl and mix until combined. Leave at room temperature for immediate spreading, or cover and place in the fridge until ready to use.

7 When ready to serve, sprinkle the top of the butter with the black pepper and some sea salt.

NOTE

Only ½ cup of the butter needs to be softened. To ensure it's as easy to work with as possible, take the butter out of the fridge the night before.

BROCCOLINI
WITH BLACK GARLIC SALSA VERDE

Kosher salt

1 pound (454 grams) fresh broccolini

2 cups (50 grams) fresh parsley leaves, finely chopped

2 to 3 Black Garlic cloves (page 65), peeled and finely chopped (3 tablespoons)

1 large spoonful of Pickled Red Onions (page 55), finely chopped (3 tablespoons)

1 Preserved Lemon (page 51), finely chopped (2 tablespoons)

1 fresh Fresno chile, finely chopped (1 tablespoon)

¼ cup (59 milliliters) extra-virgin olive oil, plus more for cooking

1 teaspoon sherry vinegar

Freshly ground black pepper

1 garlic clove, smashed

1 lemon, halved

While most people associate salsa verde with Mexican food, this nontraditional use is more Italian inspired. My version includes various pickles, preserves, and fermentations to add layers of complexity to a familiar sauce.

1 Bring a large pot of salted water to a boil over high heat. Prepare an ice bath in a large bowl.

2 Blanch the broccolini for 30 seconds, then dunk into the ice bath. Remove from the ice bath and lay out the broccolini on a tray or plate to dry.

3 Place the parsley, black garlic, pickled red onion, preserved lemon, and Fresno chile in a medium bowl. Add the ¼ cup olive oil and the sherry vinegar and mix well. Taste and adjust the seasoning with salt and pepper, if needed.

4 Heat a large sauté pan (or shallow straight-sided pan) over medium-high heat and add a few tablespoons of olive oil. When the oil shimmers and begins to smoke, add the blanched broccolini and season with some salt. Cook 2 minutes, until you have a nice color on one side, then flip the broccolini. Add the garlic and more olive oil, if needed, and continue to cook for 1 to 2 minutes. When the broccolini has a good color on both sides, add a squeeze of lemon juice.

5 Arrange the broccolini on a serving platter and top with the salsa verde, then serve.

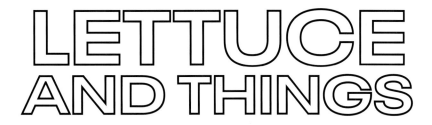

LETTUCE AND THINGS

SALADS TO WRITE HOME ABOUT. WITH THESE RECIPES, THE DEVIL IS IN THE DETAILS—AN UNEXPECTED TECHNIQUE, A CREAMY, DREAMY HOMEMADE CHEESE, A DUSTING OF BURNT ONION POWDER, OR A GAME-CHANGING BRINE.

BLISTERED GRAPES
WITH STRACCIATELLA AND SABA

8 ounces (227 grams) seedless red grapes

1 garlic clove

2 tablespoons Marcona almonds

1 tablespoon extra-virgin olive oil, plus more for drizzling

1 fresh rosemary sprig

Kosher salt

6 ounces (170 grams) stracciatella cheese (see Note)

Freshly ground black pepper

2 ounces (57 grams) mesclun mix

Chardonnay vinegar

1 tablespoon saba

I once posted a TikTok video that featured some roasted grapes, and the number of questions I got as a result was incredible. *Why would you cook a grape?* everyone wanted to know. Here's the deal. A blistered grape gets caramelized on the outside and has a jelly-like texture inside. Pair that with saba (cooked grape must, the precursor to balsamic vinegar) and some savory elements like rosemary and cheese, and you've got yourself a fine salad.

1 Discard any stems from the grapes. Smash the garlic clove. Chop the almonds.

2 Heat the tablespoon of olive oil in a large sauté pan (or shallow straight-sided pan) over high heat. When the oil is shimmering, add the grapes and blister for 1 minute. Add the garlic, then the rosemary and a pinch of salt. Continue to cook, shaking the pan every minute or so, until the grapes are blistered on all sides, about 4 minutes total. Transfer the grapes to a plate or bowl to cool completely.

3 Season the cheese with salt and pepper. Place the mesclun mix in a large bowl and lightly dress with the vinegar and olive oil. Season to taste with salt and pepper.

4 Spread the cheese in the bottom of a large serving bowl. (Alternatively, divide the cheese among 4 bowls.) Arrange the blistered grapes on top of the cheese, followed by the chopped almonds and the mesclun. Drizzle the saba on top and serve immediately.

NOTE

Stracciatella cheese is a creamy fresh Italian cheese made of small mozzarella curds mixed with fresh cream. It's also used to stuff burrata.

LITTLE GEMS
WITH CRÈME FRAÎCHE, BURNT ONION, AND SEEDS

2 heads of Little Gem lettuce

½ cup (8 grams) fresh parsley leaves (no stems)

1 small bunch fresh chives

½ cup (8 grams) fresh dill leaves (no stems), plus more for garnish

2 garlic cloves

1 medium lemon

8 ounces (227 grams) crème fraîche

2 tablespoons Burnt Onion Powder (page 27), plus more for garnish

Kosher salt and freshly ground black pepper

¼ cup (80 grams) Sweet Pickled Shallots (page 60)

¼ cup (about 28 grams) All the Seeds Mix (page 30)

SPECIAL EQUIPMENT:

salad spinner, Microplane or other grater

All right, this salad was born out of a busy night on the line. We were in the middle of the dinner rush and a child asked for ranch dressing—which was odd because I couldn't think of anything on the menu that would taste good with ranch. We definitely didn't have a bottle of Hidden Valley lying around, so I opened my lowboy and threw this together (minus the burnt onion). And it tasted pretty great.

The base for ranch dressing is mayo with buttermilk, sour cream, or both. But crème fraîche actually makes sense as a substitute. It's a European-style cultured cream that's a little higher in fat, rendering it creamier and richer. After that night, every now and then I'd be asked to make "fancy ranch" on the fly. So, here's a wedge salad with said fancy ranch, plus a little burnt onion powder, sweet pickled shallots, and the best mix of seeds.

1   To clean the lettuces, remove a couple of the outer leaves if they're soggy and cut them in half. Place them in a small bowl with a little water and a few ice cubes, and soak for 30 minutes. Using a salad spinner, dry the leaves, placing them face down in the spinner to encourage any leftover water to drip out.

2   Meanwhile, finely chop the parsley, chives, and dill, then add to a small bowl. Using a Microplane, grate the garlic and then zest the lemon into the bowl. Juice enough of the lemon to capture 1 tablespoon juice. Add this to the bowl, too.

3   To the same bowl, add the crème fraîche and onion powder. Whisk lightly and taste, adding salt and pepper as needed. Cover and store the dressing in the fridge until you're ready to use.

4   To assemble the salad, add a few tablespoons of the dressing to a small bowl. Press the lettuces cut side down into the dressing. Really try to force the dressing between the leaves, adding more dressing as needed. Flip the lettuces over and dress the undersides.

5   Arrange the lettuces on 2 serving plates and top each with a sprinkling of the seed mix, plus a few sprigs of dill, the shallots, and a dusting of the onion powder. Serve at once.

LETTUCE AND THINGS

135

BEET SALAD, CHEVRE, AND PISTACHIO

FOR THE BEETS

¼ cup unsalted shelled raw pistachios

Extra-virgin olive oil

2 tablespoons kosher salt, plus more for seasoning

1 bunch candy-stripe fresh beets (or red beets)

1 bunch fresh golden beets

¼ cup (59 milliliters) water

3 cups (750 milliliters) tangerine juice

¼ cup (59 milliliters) Champagne vinegar

3 tablespoons granulated sugar

Kosher salt

FOR THE SALAD

8 ounces (223 grams) chevre (goat cheese)

1 lemon

Kosher salt

1 Cara Cara orange

1 blood orange

Pistachio oil

1 handful of microgreens, preferably radish sprouts or nasturtium

This dish is pretty special for me. Back when I was a younger line cook, I was fortunate to work under a chef who gave me and everyone else in the kitchen a lot of creative freedom. If we had an idea for something tasty, we could bring it to the chef, and if he liked it, we would work on it until it was a dish for the menu.

This was my first dish to get on a menu, and it was my first step in finding my own food voice. Beets and goat cheese is a combo so classic that it's almost cliché. But I wanted to put my own spin on it— something bright and fresh, and nothing like the bland versions I'd had before. So, I used four different types of citrus (it's actually almost more of a citrus salad), plus salty cheese, lots of acid, peppery herbs, and pistachios to tie everything together.

ROAST AND MARINATE THE BEETS (1 DAY AHEAD)

1   Preheat the oven to 350°F (177°C).

2   Lightly dress the pistachios with some olive oil and season with some salt. Spread in a single layer on a quarter sheet pan and roast for 8 minutes, until toasted. Let cool, then roughly chop.

3   Remove the greens from the beets and reserve for another use. Rinse the beets under running water. Pick out the smallest beet and set aside for garnish shaving.

4   Place the beets in a medium baking dish. Add a few tablespoons of olive oil and the water. Cover the top tightly with aluminum foil and roast for 1 hour, until the beets can be easily pierced with a sharp object. Let cool completely.

5   Meanwhile, make the brine. Combine the tangerine juice, vinegar, sugar, and 2 tablespoons of the salt in a large bowl or liquid measuring cup and whisk until everything is fully dissolved.

6   Keeping the two different types of beet separate (or not, if you don't mind their colors bleeding together—it'll still taste delicious), peel the beets. The skins will slip right off under your fingers. Trim the stem end from each beet and cut the beets into quarters. (If your beets are large, cut them into bite-sized pieces.)

7   Divide the cut beets among jars or airtight containers, still keeping the colors separated. Pour the brine over the beets, cover, and refrigerate overnight to marinate.

SPECIAL EQUIPMENT:

Microplane or other
grater (optional),
mandoline (optional)

ASSEMBLE THE SALAD AND SERVE

1   Place the goat cheese in a medium mixing bowl. Use a Microplane to zest the lemon into the bowl. Squeeze half the lemon, then add approximately 2 teaspoons lemon juice to the bowl. Keeping in mind that goat cheese is pretty salty already, taste and season with salt, if necessary. Using a whisk or fork, whip the goat cheese until smooth and spreadable. Keep in the fridge until you're ready to serve.

2   Grab that small beet you saved earlier and peel it. Using a mandoline or a sharp knife, slice it into ⅛-inch-thick slices. Place the slices in a small bowl of water to prevent them from oxidizing or drying out.

3   Next, make the citrus supremes. Slice off the top and bottom of the oranges. Working one at a time, stand each orange upright and use a small knife to follow the curve of the fruit inside the peel, removing the rind and pith. You'll now be able to see the membranes that separate the wedges. Use your knife to slice along the inside of the membranes to cut out individual wedges.

4 Right before serving, drain the shaved beet and dress with a little bit of the beet brine.

5 Spread a spoonful of goat cheese on each serving plate. Using a slotted spoon, scoop out some of the marinated beets (8 to 10 pieces per plate) and lightly drain before placing on top of the goat cheese. Place 4 to 5 citrus supremes in the blank spaces between, then add shavings of the small beet on top.

6 Sprinkle the chopped pistachios over the beets, then drizzle the salad generously with the pistachio oil. Garnish with the microgreens and serve.

TOMATO AND PEACH SALAD
WITH FARMER CHEESE AND DILL VINNY

Tomato and peach is a classic, wonderful combination. With freshly made cheese, bright herbs, and what I like to call "dill vinny," it's incredibly refreshing.

FOR THE FARMER CHEESE

1 quart (946 milliliters) whole milk

2 cups (473 milliliters) heavy cream

2 cups (473 milliliters) cultured buttermilk

2 teaspoons kosher salt

FOR THE DILL VINNY

½ cup (118 milliliters) sunflower oil, chilled for 45 minutes in freezer

⅔ cup (16 grams) packed fresh dill

Kosher salt

2 teaspoons Champagne vinegar

FOR THE SALAD

12 ounces (340 grams) cherry tomatoes

Kosher salt

Sherry vinegar

2 white peaches, halved and pits removed

Freshly ground black pepper

Flaky sea salt, such as Maldon

2 tablespoons All the Seeds Mix (page 30)

2 fresh dill sprigs, leaves only

MAKE THE FARMER CHEESE (2–3 HOURS AHEAD)

1   Add the milk, cream, and buttermilk to a medium saucepan and set over low heat. Heat, stirring occasionally, until the mixture reaches 205°F (96°C). Turn off the heat and let it sit for 30 minutes.

2   Strain the milk mixture through a chinois (or through a fine-mesh strainer lined with cheesecloth) into a large bowl. Let the milk strain for a few hours, or even better overnight in the fridge. Reserve both the curds and the whey.

3   Add the curds to the food processor along with the salt and blend until smooth and spreadable. If it tightens, add a bit of the whey to loosen it and blend again until desired consistency. Transfer the cheese to an airtight container and store in the fridge for up to 1 week.

MAKE THE DILL VINNY

1   Place the cold sunflower oil, the dill, and a pinch of salt in the blender and blend for 30 to 45 seconds, until the dill is broken down and the oil is green.

2   Stir in the vinegar. Transfer the mixture to an airtight container and store in the fridge until ready to use. (For best flavor and color, use within 3 days. It's still edible for up to 1 week, though it may start to turn brown sooner.)

MAKE THE SALAD AND SERVE

1   Quarter the cherry tomatoes and add to a medium bowl with a pinch of salt. Lightly dress with the vinegar. Let sit and marinate while you fix the rest of the salad.

2   Cut the white peaches into bite-sized pieces. Season with salt and lightly dress with some vinegar.

SPECIAL EQUIPMENT:
food processor, instant-read thermometer, chinois (optional), high-powered blender

3 Spread the farmer cheese on the bottom of a large serving platter or bowl and season with pepper and sea salt. Spread the tomatoes and white peaches evenly over the cheese, then sprinkle with the seed mix.

4 Drizzle a few spoonfuls of the dill vinny over the top of the salad in random places, then garnish with the fresh dill. Serve.

FARMERS' MARKET

Almost every restaurant I've worked in has had a special relationship with the farmers' markets scattered across Los Angeles. Get to the Santa Monica or Hollywood farmers' market early enough and you'll see chefs, CDCs (*chefs de cuisine*), and sous chefs picking out cases of produce before the busy crowds roll in. You may also catch sight of shoppers hired by restaurants slapping stickers on boxes to claim their desired produce. Most of the people there are on a first-name basis, talking about what's really good right now or what's coming in soon that they should be excited about.

But farmers' markets are not just for professionals. Everyone should frequent their local farmers' market. In an internet world where you can order everything you need without ever having to see or speak to anyone, it's pretty cool to be able to talk directly with the people who grow the food they are selling you.

In addition to enjoying the community atmosphere, going to the markets gets me excited about the seasons. Because of the way vegetables and fruits are farmed, stored, and shipped these days, most supermarket foods are available year-round. The out-of-season produce is usually harvested early, packed up for a long trip, and allowed to ripen on the way (a process that is sometimes induced by gas). Not only does this require a lot of resources but I honestly think you can taste the difference between locally grown seasonal foods and mass-processed grocery store ones. Think of a middle-of-winter strawberry—it just tastes watery. But eating seasonally really allows you to taste everything the way it was meant to be. For me, it also keeps things interesting, challenging me to flex my creativity.

A farmers' market is also a place to find produce you won't normally find in a grocery store. Come spring in LA, you'll come across green garlic, green strawberries, and all kinds of shoots and tendrils. In summer, there are varieties of squash (and their blossoms), sour cherries, and such heirlooms as Jimmy Nardello peppers. Depending on where you live, you'll find the best of what's around at a particular time—every region has specific items you'll be hard-pressed to find anywhere else.

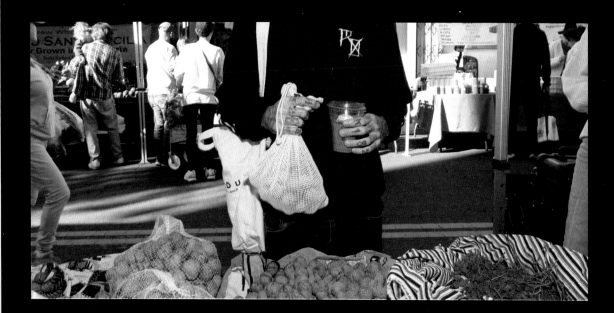

PASTAS

THE ULTIMATE COMFORT FOOD. FRESH PASTA THAT YOU MAKE WITH YOUR OWN HANDS IS UNPARALLELED. WELCOME TO THE BIG LEAGUES.

POTATO GNOCCHI

2½ pounds (1 kilogram) russet potatoes

1 cup (127 grams) 00 flour (see Note), plus more as needed

2 teaspoons kosher salt, plus more as needed

1 large egg yolk

SPECIAL EQUIPMENT:

ricer or tamis, bench scraper, pasta paddle

NOTE

The 00 flour is a very finely ground wheat flour; it may be labeled Tipo "00" if the brand is Italian. Most grocery stores now carry it.

Gnocchi are my favorite little dumplings—the potato ones specifically, because I'm a simp for most things potato. Plus, they're really versatile. With this recipe, you can portion and freeze the gnocchi ahead, then bust them out in a pinch for a quick meal.

1 Preheat the oven to 425°F (218°C).

2 Using a fork, poke holes all over the potatoes to allow steam to escape. Fit a wire rack into a half sheet pan. Lay the potatoes on the rack and roast for 45 minutes to 1 hour, until tender and easily pierced with a fork.

3 Using a paring knife, cut the potatoes in half lengthwise to release moisture and let cool for 15 minutes, or until cool enough to handle.

4 Peel the potatoes, then pass the pulp through the ricer or tamis.

5 Spread the potato mash on a clean work surface. Dust with the cup of 00 flour and the 2 teaspoons salt, then add the egg yolk. Using the bench scraper, fold the potato mash over onto itself to incorporate the flour until you have a cohesive dough. Knead for 5 minutes. The dough should be pretty smooth and soft, but not at all like a pasta dough that springs back when you poke it.

6 Cut the ball of dough in half. Using a rolling pin, roll one half into a large, ¼-inch-thick rectangular sheet. Using the bench scraper, cut the dough into ½-inch-wide strips.

7 Roll the dough strips underneath your palms until they are smooth logs, then use the bench scraper to cut them into little "pillows" about ½ inch long. Dust lightly with a little flour and set aside. Repeat with the remaining half piece of dough.

8 Using preferably a pasta paddle or the back of a fork, use one finger to roll a dough pillow across the paddle surface with even pressure to create grooves on one side and an indentation on the other side. Repeat with remaining dough pillows.

9 Bring a large pot of salted water to a boil. Working in batches, gently add the gnocchi to the pot and cook for about 1 minute, or 30 seconds after they begin to float to the surface. Scoop out the cooked gnocchi with a slotted spoon.

10 If serving immediately, drop the cooked gnocchi directly into your sauce. Alternatively, lay the cooked gnocchi on an oiled tray or platter to cool. Cover and store in the fridge for up to 1 week or freeze for 1 month.

POTATO GNOCCHI WITH CHILE POMODORO AND FRIED GARLIC

6 garlic cloves

½ cup (118 milliliters) sunflower oil

Fine sea salt

1 tablespoon extra-virgin olive oil

½ recipe Potato Gnocchi (page 157)

3 cups (720 milliliters) Chile Pomodoro (page 80)

4 ounces (56 grams) Parmesan cheese, shaved

Fresh basil leaves, for garnish

It looks like a simple plate of gnocchi and marinara, but it's so much more. Pillowy homemade gnocchi, garlicky pomodoro with a warm kick from Fresno chiles, and fried garlic crisps without bite. Perfection doesn't even begin to cover it.

1   Put the garlic in a small saucepan. Cover with cold water and place over medium heat. Bring to a boil, then immediately strain off the water and add fresh cold water. Return to a boil over medium heat, then strain off the water again. Repeat one more time. (This triple blanching of the garlic breaks down the compounds that contribute to garlic's smelly pungency and leaves the garlic sweet and mild.) Place the garlic in a small bowl and cover with cold water; let cool completely. When cool, remove from the water and dry the garlic.

2   Slice off the root end from each garlic clove. Slice the garlic lengthwise into ⅛-inch-thick slices.

3   Place the garlic slivers in a small saucepan. Cover with the sunflower oil and place over medium heat. Gently fry the garlic until light golden brown, 3 to 4 minutes. Avoid letting it turn deep golden brown, as the garlic will continue to cook even after it's removed from the heat. Scoop the garlic from the oil and place on a paper towel to drain. Season with a pinch of the salt.

4   Heat a large saucepan over medium-high heat and add the olive oil. When the oil is shimmering and starting to smoke, add the gnocchi in a single layer. Add a small pinch of salt and allow the gnocchi to cook until they are nicely seared on one side. Jiggle the pan to reposition them and add the chile pomodoro.

5   Heat the pomodoro through, then taste and adjust seasoning, if needed. Place the gnocchi and sauce on individual plates and top each with some of the shaved Parmesan. Sprinkle with the fried garlic, and then the fresh basil. Serve at once.

TAGLIATELLE

3 large eggs, at room temperature

2 large egg yolks, at room temperature

2 cups (288 grams) 00 flour (see Note on page 157), plus more as needed

1 teaspoon kosher salt

1 teaspoon extra-virgin olive oil

Semolina flour, for storing cut pasta

SPECIAL EQUIPMENT:

bench scraper, pasta roller (optional)

This recipe, which calls for whole eggs plus additional egg yolks, has become my universal pasta dough. The egg whites are mostly water and make the dough more forgiving, and therefore easier to work with; the extra egg yolks add color and richness. You can roll out and cut the pasta dough by hand or use a pasta machine. Beyond tagliatelle, the dough is great for a variety of pasta types, even for a filled pasta like agnolotti.

MAKE THE DOUGH

1 Place the eggs and egg yolks in a medium bowl and whisk lightly.

2 Pour the 2 cups flour into a mound on a clean work surface. Use the underside of the bowl to create a well in the center. Carefully pour the eggs into the well, then add the salt and olive oil. Use a fork to whisk the eggs in a circular motion, gently pulling the flour into the center. When you have what resembles a loose batter, start flicking the flour from the edge of the well into the center while avoiding breaking the wall itself. When you have a thick batter, use the bench scraper to begin scooping the flour onto the batter, almost as if you're kneading it. Do this until the dough comes together in a ball.

3 Knead the dough for 10 to 15 minutes, until very smooth, almost an elastic ball. A good way to check is to poke the dough with your finger. It should gently bounce back. Place the dough in a large bowl and cover with a clean kitchen cloth. Let rest for 30 to 45 minutes. If you try to work with it and it starts springing back and resisting you, let it rest another 15 minutes. (You can also wrap the dough in plastic wrap and let it rest in the fridge for up to 2 days. It's a lot easier to roll and shape the pasta if it's well rested.)

TO CUT THE DOUGH BY HAND

1 Dust a half sheet pan with some semolina flour.

2 Lightly flour a large work surface and cut the dough into 4 pieces to make it easier to work with. Shape 1 piece of dough into a little ball and press it down with your palm so it's a small circle. Begin rolling the dough outward from the center until you have a narrow rectangular sheet at least 12 inches long and 1/8 inch thick or less. Lightly flour the pasta sheet and repeat with the next piece of dough, then the remaining 2 pieces. (If you don't have a large enough work surface, roll the dough in batches.)

PASTAS

161

3 Working with one sheet of pasta at a time, fold one end of the pasta sheet over itself into the middle; repeat with the other end. The ends of both folds should meet in the middle. Use a sharp knife to cut the pasta into strips about ¼ inch wide. Slide your knife underneath the pasta in the middle where the ends meet and lift the strips up, giving them a gentle shake to unroll the pasta. Repeat with the remaining 3 sheets of dough.

4 Wrap the pasta strips around your hand to create nests. Set them on the sheet pan dusted with the semolina.

TO USE A PASTA MACHINE

1 Lightly flour a clean work surface. Dust a half sheet pan with the semolina flour.

2 Cut the dough into 4 pieces. Using your hands, shape each dough wedge into an oval. Feed one of the ovals at a time through the pasta maker on the widest setting. For me, that's number 1. When it passes through the rollers, fold the dough into thirds, similar to a letter fold. Feed that sheet through the rollers 2 or 3 more times, still on the widest setting.

3 Continue to feed the dough through the rollers as you gradually reduce the settings, one pass at a time, until the pasta reaches your desired thickness. For my machine it's number 6. Whenever the dough starts to get a bit sticky, just pause and drape the dough over the floured surface to reflour it, being sure to coat both sides. If the dough sheet starts to get too long to handle, just cut it into 2 pieces.

4 When dough is desired thickness, sprinkle it with a bit more flour once again. Connect the cutter attachment to your pasta maker and feed the sheet through to cut the tagliatelle. Wrap the cut pasta around your hand as it emerges from the machine, creating a little nest. Set it on the sheet pan and repeat with the remaining 3 pasta ovals.

TO STORE AND COOK (EITHER METHOD)

1 Cover the pasta and keep it in the fridge, using it within 3 days. To freeze the fresh pasta, toss it with more semolina and place in an airtight container, storing it for up to 1 month.

2 To cook the fresh pasta, drop it into boiling salted water and cook until al dente, about 3 minutes. If cooking from frozen, the pasta may need an extra 1 to 2 minutes to cook. Drain and mix the pasta into your sauce just before serving.

TAGLIATELLE AND MORELS

4 cups (600 grams) fresh morel mushrooms

3 cups (750 milliliters) Mushroom Stock (page 88)

Kosher salt

1 pound (453 grams) Tagliatelle (page 161)

4 medium shallots

4 garlic cloves

¼ cup (59 milliliters) extra-virgin olive oil

½ cup (1 stick; 113 grams) unsalted butter

4 teaspoons fresh thyme leaves

¼ cup (59 milliliters) dry white wine

4 ounces (56 grams) Parmesan cheese, freshly grated

Freshly ground black pepper

Fresh morels are my favorite type of mushroom. They're pricey, but worth the splurge if you can swing it. Morels usually are in season between March and June, but if you can't find them in your grocery store, swap in any other mushroom of choice. In this case, my next choice would be maitake mushrooms, which you don't have to poach; just go directly to the sauté step, then follow the remaining instructions.

POACH THE MUSHROOMS

1   Wash the morels, then cut them in half (or quarters, if they are large).

2   Add the stock to a large saucepan and bring to a simmer over low heat. Add the morels and simmer about 15 minutes, until al dente. They should still have quite a nice bite to them—morels are hearty that way. Spread out the morels on a tray or plate to dry. Reserve the now-fortified stock.

COOK THE PASTA

1   Bring a large pot of salted water to a boil over high heat.

2   Add the pasta and cook about 3 minutes, until al dente. Drain the pasta. Reserve 1 cup of the pasta water.

COMBINE AND SERVE

1   Finely mince the shallots and garlic.

2   Heat a large sauté pan (or shallow straight-sided pan) over medium-high heat. Add the olive oil and 4 tablespoons of the butter. When the butter has melted and is foaming, add the morels and a small pinch of salt. Cook about 4 minutes, until the morels have a nice sear on one side. Stir in the shallots and garlic and cook about 2 minutes more, stirring, until the shallots are translucent.

3   Add the thyme and stir in the wine to deglaze the pan. When the wine is almost gone, add ¼ cup of the fortified stock. Stir in the pasta and add a splash of the pasta-cooking water. Reduce the heat to low and add the remaining 4 tablespoons butter. Toss to combine well, then add half the grated cheese and toss again to incorporate.

4   If the pasta looks dry, add a splash more of the fortified stock and toss to achieve a nice sauce. Taste and season with salt and pepper.

5   Divide the pasta among 4 bowls or plates and top each serving with some of the mushrooms and the remaining cheese.

MAINS

THE MAIN EVENT. AND THE CHAPTER YOU'LL REPEATEDLY TURN TO WHEN YOU REALLY WANT TO IMPRESS. SOME OF THESE RECIPES TAKE ALL DAY TO PRE-PARE. HELL, SOME REQUIRE MULTIPLE DAYS. BUT I PROMISE YOU THAT THE EFFORT WILL BE WORTH IT. YOU (YES, YOU!) ARE TOTALLY CAPABLE OF CREAT-ING A BEAUTIFUL, COMPLEX MEAL WORTHY OF A FANCY RESTAURANT.

ROAST CHICKEN AND JUS

1 chicken, approximately 4 pounds (1.8 kilograms), neck and giblets removed

3 fresh rosemary sprigs

10 fresh thyme sprigs

1 tablespoon kosher salt, plus more for seasoning

Neutral oil, such as sunflower, grapeseed, or vegetable

4 small shallots

1 bulb of garlic

1½ quarts (1.4 liters) Dark Chicken Stock (page 85)

2 tablespoons brandy

1 fresh bay leaf (or 2 dried)

1 tablespoon cold unsalted butter

Finely ground black pepper

Extra-virgin olive oil

SPECIAL EQUIPMENT:

kitchen shears, instant-read thermometer

A roasted chicken may not sound impressive, but if done right, it's top tier. A dry-brined, perfectly roasted bird with crispy golden skin and a shiny pan sauce—that's a chef's kiss. To be honest, I skip the holiday turkeys and make this instead.

PREPARE THE CHICKEN (1 DAY AHEAD)

1 Position the chicken breast side up on a cutting board, with the neck end facing you. Feel around the neck opening to locate the wishbone. Using the tip of a knife to cut around the wishbone, insert your fingers to pull it out.

2 Flip the chicken over so it is breast side down. Using kitchen shears, cut along either side of the backbone to remove it. Set the backbone aside for later use in the jus. Flip the chicken so it is breast side up again and press down on the sternum to flatten it.

3 Finely chop all the rosemary and 5 sprigs of the thyme. Rub the herbs underneath the skin and on the underside of the bird. Season the chicken with the tablespoon of salt.

4 Fit a wire rack into a half sheet pan. Place the chicken on the rack and set, uncovered, in the fridge to dry-brine overnight or up to 24 hours.

COOK THE JUS (SAME DAY)

1 Chop the backbone of the chicken into 1-inch pieces. Slice the shallots about ¼ inch thick. Cut off the root end from the bulb of garlic, then cut the bulb in half horizontally so you have 2 pieces held together by the skins.

2 Place the stock in a large pot over low heat to warm.

3 Heat a large sauté pan (or shallow straight-sided pan), or a medium saucepan, over medium-high heat. Add a couple tablespoons of the oil. When it shimmers and begins to smoke, add the back pieces and brown evenly on all sides about 2 minutes per side.

4 Add the garlic, cut sides down, and begin to brown for 2 minutes in the oil until golden. Add the shallots and cook about 3 minutes, stirring often, until translucent.

5   Add the brandy to the pan and scrape the bottom with a rubber spatula to release the browned bits (*fond*). When the brandy is almost evaporated, add the warm stock, the remaining 5 sprigs of thyme, and the bay leaf. Bring to a simmer and then cook about 45 minutes to reduce by just over half, every so often skimming any fat or foam that forms on the surface. Use a rubber spatula to clean the sides of the pot to incorporate that sticky liquid back into the sauce.

6   Strain the liquid into a medium saucepan. Continue to reduce for 30 to 45 minutes, until the liquid is *nappe* (coats the back of a spoon). To check consistency, pour a small amount of the sauce onto a plate. It shouldn't be watery and should hold its shape. When you're satisfied with the consistency, whisk in the cold butter. Taste and adjust the seasoning with salt and black pepper.

7   Cover the jus, reduce the heat to very low, and keep warm until ready to serve.

ROAST THE CHICKEN AND SERVE

1   Preheat the oven to 425°F (218°C).

2   Brush the skin of the chicken with some of the olive oil. Roast until the thickest part of the breast reaches 155°F (68°C), about 45 minutes. Remove from the oven, cover lightly with foil, and let rest for 20 minutes.

3   To serve, remove the legs from the chicken and carve the breast from the bone. Arrange the chicken pieces on 4 to 6 individual plates and then spoon a generous serving of jus over each portion. Serve.

NOTE

The deal with dry brining: Instead of submerging the bird in a ton of water, dry brining uses the moisture from the chicken to create a brine that will be reabsorbed into the meat before cooking. Letting the chicken hang out overnight in the fridge allows the salt to more evenly and effectively season the meat. It'll also lead to crispier, more crackly skin.

DUCK CONFIT
WITH MOLE POBLANO

Mole poblano, one of my favorite foods ever, is regarded as the national dish of Mexico. The sauce is usually served with chicken or turkey, but this mashup is influenced by my French culinary training. The recipe yields a lot of mole sauce (4 cups). You can easily increase the number of thighs to serve more people, or freeze any extra sauce to use later on.

FOR THE DUCK CONFIT

2 tablespoons kosher salt

1 teaspoon ground coriander

½ teaspoon ground black pepper

4 duck legs, approximately 2 pounds (1 kilogram)

¼ cup duck fat

FOR THE MOLE POBLANO

5 dried ancho chiles

4 dried guajillo chiles

4 dried chiles de arbol

1 quart (946 milliliters) Dark Chicken Stock (page 85)

3 garlic cloves

½ large white onion

2 teaspoons coriander seeds

1 teaspoon cumin seeds

4 whole cloves

3 black peppercorns

1 1-inch piece cinnamon stick

Neutral oil, such as sunflower, grapeseed, or vegetable

½ cup (71 grams) unsalted raw almonds

½ cup (62 grams) unsalted raw peanuts

¼ cup (29 grams) unsalted pepitas

¼ cup white sesame seeds, plus more for garnish

½ cup black raisins

¼ cup torn pieces of bolillo or white bread

1 disc (93 grams) Mexican chocolate, or more as desired

Kosher salt

Piloncillo (optional; see Note)

SPECIAL EQUIPMENT:

Cryovac (vacuum-pack) bag, sous vide water circulator, high-powered blender

MAKE THE DUCK CONFIT (2 DAYS AHEAD)

1 Place the salt, coriander, and pepper in a small bowl and stir until combined. Rub the mix all over the duck legs. Fit a small wire rack into a quarter sheet pan. Place the legs on the rack and set, uncovered, overnight in the fridge to dry-brine.

2 The next day, add the duck legs to a Cryovac (vacuum-pack) bag, along with the duck fat. Seal according to manufacturer's instructions.

MAINS

173

3 Heat a water bath with a sous vide water circulator set to 155°F (68°C). Add the packet of duck legs and let cook for 24 hours.

4 When you're almost ready to pull out the duck legs, prepare an ice bath in a large bowl. Place the duck legs in the ice bath to halt the cooking and cool them down. (You can prepare ahead and store the duck legs in the fridge for up to 1 week.)

MAKE THE MOLE POBLANO (SAME DAY)

1 Remove the stems, ribs, and seeds from the dried ancho and guajillo chiles. Reserve the seeds and chiles separately. Leave the chiles de arbol whole.

2 Heat a dry sauté pan over medium-high heat. Working in batches if necessary, toast the chiles in the hot pan for 1 to 2 minutes, until they get a nice brown color and are slightly blistered. Transfer to a small bowl.

3 Add the chile seeds to the pan and toast lightly, about 1 minute.

4 Return the chiles to the pan and add 1 cup of the stock. Bring to a gentle boil over medium-high heat, then reduce the heat to low and simmer for 15 minutes, until the chiles are soft and pliable. Transfer the chiles to the blender but do not process.

5 Heat the remaining 3 cups stock in a large saucepan over low heat and keep warm.

6 Smash the garlic cloves. Slice the onion into ¼-inch-thick rounds.

7 Heat a large sauté pan (or shallow straight-sided pan) over medium-low heat. Add the coriander seeds, cumin seeds, cloves, peppercorns, and cinnamon stick. Toast about 3 minutes, shaking the pan often, until fragrant. Transfer to a small bowl.

8 In the same pan over medium-low heat, add a few tablespoons of the oil. Add the almonds and toast for 4 minutes, stirring often. Add the peanuts and toast for an additional 4 minutes, stirring often, then add the pepitas and toast for 4 more minutes, stirring often. Everything should be deeper in color and very fragrant. Spread on a plate or tray to cool.

9 Add the sesame seeds and toast about 5 minutes, stirring constantly, until golden. Add to the nuts.

10 Add a couple tablespoons more of the oil to the pan, then add the raisins. Cook about 5 minutes, stirring often, until the raisins are blistered. Transfer to a medium bowl.

11 Add the garlic cloves to the pan and shallow-fry for 2 minutes, until golden. Next, add the onion rounds and cook about 5 minutes, tossing occasionally, until they have gained some color. Add to the raisins in the bowl.

12 Lastly, add the bread pieces to the pan and toast for 3 minutes, until golden all over. Add to the raisins, onion, and garlic.

13 Now, begin blending. First, using the blender, process the chiles with the toasted spices until you have a smooth, thick paste. Add stock as needed to help it spin, but don't add too much in the beginning. Use a rubber spatula to scrape down the sides of the blender frequently.

14 Add the disc of Mexican chocolate and blend until smooth. Add the nuts, seeds, and some more stock (about 1 cup), and blend until smooth.

15 Lastly, add the raisins, onions, garlic, bread bits, and a touch more broth to the blender and blend until smooth. Transfer the mole to a medium saucepan. Add a little stock to the blender and give it a quick pulse to pick up everything left behind, then pour it into the mole.

16 Taste and adjust the seasoning with salt, additional chocolate if desired, and/or the piloncillo, if using. If you need to thin the sauce, stir in a touch more stock. Keep warm.

FINISH THE DISH AND SERVE

1 Preheat the broiler on low (350°F).

2 Place the duck legs under the broiler for 8 to 10 minutes, until the skin is crispy. (Alternatively, heat a medium saucepan over medium-low heat, add the duck legs, and render the fat under its skin, about 8 minutes. You're going to have to move the legs around and stand them up against the sides of the pan to render all the fat evenly. Drain any excess fat if you need to. Remember, the duck is already cooked, so you're just crisping up the skin and warming it through.)

3 Place the legs on a serving platter, spoon over the mole poblano, and top with the extra sesame seeds.

NOTE

Piloncillo is unrefined cane sugar, sometimes called Mexican brown sugar because of its caramel notes. It's common in Mexican cooking and is nice to have on hand when making this recipe in case you feel like extra sweetness would be nice in the sauce.

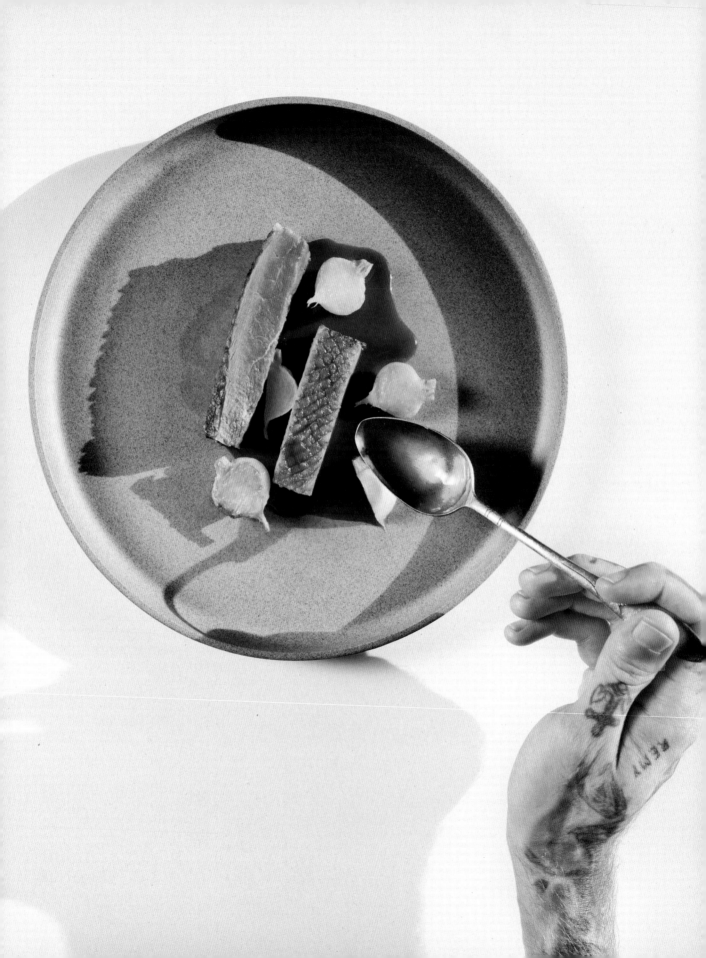

DUCK BREAST AND BRAISED TURNIPS
WITH DUCK JUS

2 8-ounce (226 grams) duck breasts

8 ounces (226 grams) baby turnips, trimmed of any greens

2 cups (473 milliliters) Blond Chicken Stock (page 84)

1 tablespoon duck fat

Kosher salt and finely ground black pepper

1 garlic clove, smashed

2 tablespoons unsalted butter

5 fresh thyme sprigs

3 fresh rosemary sprigs

2 tablespoons fresh orange juice (from ½ orange)

Duck Jus (page 86)

Flaky sea salt, such as Maldon

SPECIAL EQUIPMENT:

instant-read thermometer

This is probably one of the most restaurant-y recipes in the book. It's a plate with slices of duck breast, a few turnips, and some sauce. That'll be $99, please. But seriously—if you buy a whole duck, it's super possible to make it fancy at home.

PREP THE DUCK (2–3 HOURS AHEAD)

1 Let the duck breasts rest, uncovered, skin side up in the fridge for a few hours or up to overnight. This will help the skin dry to render nicely and get a bit crispier.

2 While the duck breasts are still cold, score a crosshatch pattern in the skin to assist in rendering the fat beneath, being careful not to cut all the way through to the meat. (It's also good for aesthetics.) Doing this while the skin is still cold will give you cleaner cuts because it is firmer.

3 Let the duck breasts come closer to room temperature about 30 minutes prior to cooking.

COOK THE TURNIPS

1 Using a peeler, peel the turnips from the stem end down to the tip. (Peeling from stem to tip helps keep their natural shape.) Cut the turnips in half vertically and place in a bowl of water.

2 Place the stock in a small saucepan over low heat and keep warm.

3 Heat a large sauté pan (or shallow straight-sided pan) over medium-low heat. Add the duck fat. When the fat is shimmering, add the turnips cut side down. Season with a small pinch of salt and cook the turnips about 5 minutes, until you have a golden-brown sear.

4 Add the garlic, butter, thyme, and rosemary. Cook for 2 minutes, until the butter browns and smells nutty. Stir in ¼ cup of the warm stock to deglaze the pan. (A 2-ounce ladle is great for this.) Continue to simmer for a few minutes, until the stock is almost gone and has become glazy and syrupy. Add another ¼ cup stock, and when the stock is almost gone again, check to see if a turnip is ready to flip over by prodding the cut side with a knife or cake tester. It should be just tender but by no means mushy. (If it's still firm, add another ¼ cup stock and continue cooking until tender.) Flip the turnips over and continue cooking for about 5 minutes, adding stock as it reduces, until the turnips are tender throughout.

5 Pick out the herb sprigs and garlic from the saucepan and add the orange juice. Taste and season with salt and pepper. Add a touch more stock and swirl the pan until you have a nice buttery glaze. Transfer the mixture to a small saucepan and cover to keep warm.

COOK THE DUCK

1 Season the duck breasts with salt on the meat side only. Lay the breasts in a large cold sauté pan skin side down. Set over low heat to gradually warm. When you see some fat trickling out from below the skin, turn the heat up to medium-low and continue rendering the fat. Keep the duck at a gentle sizzle; it shouldn't be so hot that it smokes and the skin burns before the breast is cooked. (If the heat is too low, a gray band will develop under the skin of overcooked meat.) A lot of fat is going to render out of these duck breasts, so have a container nearby to hold some of it, spooning fat out of the pan as necessary.

2   When the duck skin is browned, turn the breasts over and cook on the flesh side to your desired doneness. I serve my duck medium—an instant-read thermometer inserted into the thickest part registers 135°F (57°C). Transfer the duck to a platter and allow it to rest, skin side up, for 10 minutes, until the internal temperature rises to 140°F (60°C) for medium. For medium-rare, you're aiming for an internal temperature of 130°F (54°C) and will need to pull the duck sooner.

ASSEMBLE THE DISH AND SERVE

1   Warm the duck jus in a small saucepan.

2   Cut the duck breasts in half lengthwise, then season with pepper and a touch of sea salt. Arrange the breasts on 2 individual plates, pour a couple of spoonfuls of the jus around them, and place some turnips on the side. Serve immediately.

FOR THE BONE MARROW

2 pieces (1 pound/453 grams) beef marrow bones, canoe cut preferred (see Note)

2 quarts (1.9 liters) water

Kosher salt

FOR THE POMME PUREE

1½ pounds (600 grams) small Yukon Gold potatoes

¾ cup (177 milliliters) heavy cream

2 fresh thyme sprigs

1 garlic clove

3 ounces (80 grams) Gruyère cheese

2 tablespoons cold unsalted butter

Kosher salt and ground white pepper

FOR THE STEAK

Steak of choice (see Note)

Neutral oil, such as sunflower, grapeseed, or vegetable

Kosher salt

1 tablespoon chopped fresh parsley leaves, for garnish

Bordelaise (page 90)

Freshly ground black pepper

SPECIAL EQUIPMENT:

Microplane or other grater, food mill or ricer, instant-read thermometer

BEEF AND POMME PUREE
WITH BONE MARROW AND BORDELAISE

This is my version of "meat and potatoes"—a phrase implying it's basic or simple. Yeah, allow me to step in and make it complicated.

PREPARE THE MARROW BONES (1 DAY AHEAD)

1 Place the marrow bones in a container large enough to hold them and the water. Add salt to the water and pour over the marrow bones to cover.

2 Refrigerate the container for 24 hours, changing the water once during that time.

COOK THE MARROW BONES (NEXT DAY)

1 Preheat the oven to 450°F (232°C).

2 Remove the marrow bones from the salt solution and pat dry. Fit a wire rack on a half sheet pan and lay the bones on the rack with the marrow facing up. Roast for 18 to 20 minutes, until a cake tester or fork goes into the thickest part of the marrow with no resistance and there are no visible pink spots on the surface. Let cool to room temperature.

3 Using an offset spatula or a spoon, scoop the bone marrow away from the bones, trying to keep it as intact as possible. Lay the marrow on a small plate and place in the fridge to firm up while you cook the potatoes.

4 Cut the marrow into ¼-inch cubes and return to the fridge until ready to use.

MAKE THE POMME PUREE

1   Place the whole potatoes in a large pot and cover with cold water. Bring to a boil over medium-high heat and cook about 30 minutes, until easily pierced with a cake tester or fork.

2   While the potatoes are cooking, combine the cream and thyme sprigs in a small saucepan. Using a Microplane, grate the garlic into the cream. Place the saucepan on your smallest burner over low heat and steep the garlic in the cream until you need it; it shouldn't come to a boil or simmer but instead the heat will tame the garlic and infuse the cream with flavor.

3   Grate the cheese.

4   Drain the water from the potatoes and let cool slightly. Keep the pot nearby. Use your hands to slip the skins off the potatoes. Then pass the potatoes through a food mill or ricer and return to the pot.

5   Over very low heat, gently cook the potatoes for about 5 minutes, stirring gently with a rubber spatula, to evaporate any excess water. Add the butter and mix until fully incorporated. Pick out the thyme sprigs from the cream and slowly incorporate the warm cream into the potatoes. Add the cheese and stir until combined. Taste and season with salt and white pepper. Cover and keep warm. (If it ends up sitting for quite some time, you can add a touch of cream to adjust the consistency later.)

COOK THE STEAK

1   Pull the steak from the fridge 20 minutes before cooking. Brush with some oil on both sides, then season with salt.

2   Heat a large sauté pan over medium heat and add a few tablespoons of oil. When the oil is shimmering and begins to smoke, lay the steak in the pan and cook to desired doneness, about 130°F (54°C) for medium-rare. Let the steak rest while you get everything else ready.

ASSEMBLE THE DISH

1 Reheat the pomme puree if necessary.

2 Place the Bordelaise in a small saucepan and warm over low heat.

3 Gently warm the marrow by adding it to a small saucepan over very low heat; heat until just warmed through. (You don't want it to get extremely hot, as the bone marrow will render to liquid.) Lightly season the marrow with salt, and sprinkle with the chopped parsley, if using.

4 Slice the steak against the grain. Dip a brush in the bone marrow pot and brush the steak with the fat. Season with pepper and place on 4 serving plates. Add a spoonful of potatoes next to each portion and place the bone marrow on top, leaving behind any excess fat. Spoon the sauce around the perimeter of the dish and serve.

NOTES

Choose whichever cut of steak you like—rib eye, porterhouse, strip steak, T-bone, or filet mignon would all be great. A 32-ounce steak is perfect for family style.

A canoe cut is a lengthwise cut that exposes the marrow, making it easier to scoop out.

RIB STEAK AND GRILLED MUSHROOMS
WITH BEEF AND MUSHROOM REDUCTION

3½ ounces (99 grams) fresh king oyster mushrooms, cleaned

¾ cup (177 milliliters) Mushroom Stock (page 88), plus more as needed

1 pound (454 grams) cold unsalted butter, diced

1 large bone-in rib steak, at least 1½ inches thick (about 2 pounds)

Beef and Mushroom Reduction (page 87)

Kosher salt and freshly ground black pepper

SPECIAL EQUIPMENT:

instant-read thermometer

I worked in a restaurant that had a thing for large-format proteins. Think rib eye, porterhouse, veal chop, rack of pork, rack of lamb, and so on. The plates were served with one or two small accompaniments, but the huge piece of meat at the center was the star of the show. This is an homage to that practice.

POACH THE MUSHROOMS

1   Cut the mushrooms in half vertically and score a crosshatch pattern to help prevent curling later. (It'll also make them look good.)

2   Add the stock to a small saucepan over medium-high heat and simmer to reduce to ¼ cup, about 10 minutes. Then, turn the heat down to the lowest setting. Whisk in the butter a few cubes at a time, until you have a thick emulsified butter sauce (*beurre monte*).

3   Add the mushrooms to the sauce and "poach" them for about 20 minutes, until just tender enough to pierce easily with a knife. Be careful to keep the butter below 180°F (82°C), so it doesn't break. (If it does break, remove the mushrooms and whisk in 1 tablespoon of stock, and it should come back together.) Remove the poached mushrooms from the sauce and drain off any excess butter that might cause flare-ups when grilled later.

GRILL THE STEAK AND MUSHROOMS

1   Take the steak out of the fridge about 1 hour before you plan to grill. Heat a grill to very hot.

2   Place the reduction in a small saucepan over low heat and keep it warm.

3   Generously season the steak with salt. If cooking a bone-in cut, stand the meat on the bone by propping it up or holding it bone side down on the grill for 3 to 4 minutes; this allows some heat to travel up the bone so the cooking is more consistent. Then sear each side of the steak and cook to the desired doneness, about 130°F (54°C) for medium-rare (this should take about 6 to 10 minutes, depending on thickness).

4   Transfer the steak to a platter and let rest while you grill the mushrooms.

5   Season the mushrooms with salt and place them on the grill in an area with lower temperature. You don't really want to char with high heat—just a deep browning, picking up some smoke flavor along the way. The grilling time will vary based on the grill's heat source, but it should take roughly 8 minutes, flipping the mushrooms every 2 minutes. Remember, the mushrooms are already 90 percent cooked, so whenever they reach the desired color, take them off the grill.

ASSEMBLE THE DISH AND SERVE

1   Just before serving, place the meat on the hottest part of the grill to warm it through for just a few minutes.

2   Cut the meat from the bone and place the bone on a serving platter. Cut away the cap from the eye and slice it separately against the grain, then slice the eye against the grain and place both on the platter next to the bone. Top with a twist of freshly ground black pepper.

3   Place the mushrooms on the platter and generously spoon over the reduction. Serve immediately.

DUKKAH-CRUSTED LAMB RACK
WITH BURNT HONEY GASTRIQUE

¼ cup (59 milliliters) honey

1 tablespoon plus 1 teaspoon sherry vinegar

2 pounds (0.9 kilograms) frenched lamb rack

Neutral oil, such as sunflower, grapeseed, or vegetable

Kosher salt

Pistachio Dukkah (page 32)

SPECIAL EQUIPMENT:

instant-read thermometer

Lamb rack for two. Or one; I don't judge. "Honey gastrique" sounds fancy, but you're really just heating honey in a pot until it's toasty and caramelized, then adding a splash of sherry vinegar. Easy.

MAKE THE HONEY GASTRIQUE

1   Place the honey in a small saucepan with tall sides. (This helps avoid spillover when it bubbles up.) Place over medium-low heat and cook the honey about 15 minutes, until it turns a ruby brown and begins to smell nutty. It will bubble a lot, but try not to stir it—at most, just gently swirl the pot.

2   Let the honey cool for several minutes, then stir in the vinegar. If not using right away, pour into a small bowl, cover, and store in the fridge until ready to use.

COOK THE LAMB RACK

1   Preheat the oven to 375°F (190°C) and arrange the rack in the middle of the oven. Fit a wire rack in a half sheet pan.

2   If your butcher hasn't already done so, you need to remove the large fat cap on the rack. Reach toward the bottom of the rack and slide your fingers between the fat and the meat. Begin to gently peel the cap away—it peels easily at first. When you've exposed the meaty eye underneath, the fat cap will cling to the ribs and won't peel away as easily, so use your knife to make long strokes along the ribs and trim a bit of fat off the top. Discard this extra fat. Go back to the bottom of the lamb rack and find the tendon that runs along the bottom entire eye. Grab it and gently pull; it should pull away easily, but if you have any trouble, use the tip of your knife to carve around it.

3   Heat a large sauté pan over medium-high heat and add a few tablespoons of oil. When the oil shimmers and smokes, brush the lamb with more oil and season generously with salt. Lay the lamb fat side down in the pan and cook about 2 minutes, to render some of the fat until the meat is golden.

4 Sear the meaty end of the rack by holding it at an angle and standing it up in the pan for about 2 minutes to nicely brown. Then lay the rack meat side up on the rack and transfer the pan to the middle rack of the oven. Roast until a thermometer inserted in the centermost, thickest part of the meaty eye reads 125°F (51°C) for rare (pictured), 135°F (57°C) for medium-rare, and 140°F (60°C) for medium. (Alternatively, an oven's probe thermometer is helpful here.) I don't recommend cooking the rack to well-done, as the meat will be dry and tough. Let the lamb rest in the pan for 15 minutes to allow carryover cooking.

ASSEMBLE THE DISH AND SERVE

1 Spread the dukkah in a layer on a broad plate or tray. Brush the rack of lamb all over with a layer of the honey gastrique, then roll the lamb rack in the dukkah, pressing gently to make it stick.

2 Use a sharp knife to slice between the ribs and portion into chops. Arrange the chops on 2 serving plates and drizzle each with a spoonful of the remaining burnt honey.

PORK CHOP
WITH FENNEL POLLEN AND PEAR MOSTARDA

15 black peppercorns

1 tablespoon coriander seeds

1 quart (946 milliliters) water

1 bulb of garlic, root end trimmed and garlic cut in half horizontally

¼ cup plus 1 tablespoon (46 grams) kosher salt

2 tablespoons granulated sugar

10 fresh thyme sprigs

2 fresh rosemary sprigs

1 1½-pound/680-gram thick-cut bone-in pork chop

Freshly ground black pepper

Flaky sea salt, such as Maldon

Fennel pollen (see Note)

2 or 3 pieces Pear Mostarda (page 56)

SPECIAL EQUIPMENT:

instant-read thermometer

Pork and fennel pollen is one of my favorite combinations. I'm not wasting any time with tiny pinches here. When it comes to dusting it over the pork chop, I'm really liberal with the pollen. I want a complete crust. The mostarda is an added bonus—a reward.

BRINE THE PORK CHOP (4 HOURS AHEAD)

1   Add the peppercorns and coriander seeds to a medium saucepan and place over low heat. Toast about 3 minutes, until very fragrant.

2   Add 2 cups of the water and the garlic, ¼ cup salt, the sugar, and thyme and rosemary sprigs. Increase the heat to high and bring to a boil. As soon as it reaches a boil, turn off the heat and add the remaining 2 cups water to quickly cool the mix. Let cool to room temperature, then place in the fridge to chill for about an hour.

3   Place the pork chop in a large bowl and pour the brine over the chop, making sure to cover the meat. Cover the bowl and refrigerate for 2 hours.

4   Fit a wire rack in a quarter sheet pan. Remove the chop from the brine and lightly pat dry. Place on the rack and return to the fridge, uncovered, to dry the exterior. This could take upwards of 1 hour. Discard the brine.

COOK THE PORK CHOP

1   Take the pork chop out of the fridge 1 hour before you want to cook it.

2   Place a large sauté pan or carbon-steel pan over medium heat, add the pork chop cap side down, and begin to render the fat in the cap, about 2 minutes, until nicely browned. There should be some fat in the pan; you may even need to drain a bit off, depending on the thickness of the chop.

3 Lay the pork chop flat down in the fat and cook for 4 to 6 minutes, until you have a nice sear on that side. Flip, then continue to cook for 4 to 5 minutes, basting around the bone occasionally. (This is always the most difficult part to cook through.) Use an instant-read thermometer to measure the temperature of the cooked meat. The USDA has lowered the recommended temperature for cooked pork from 160°F (71°C) to 145°F (62°C), with a 5-minute rest. I recommend cooking the pork to 145°F (62°C), with the rest period having some carryover cooking. But it's your chop, so if you would like to cook it further, go right ahead. When desired temperature is reached, take the chop out of the pan and let rest for 5 minutes.

ASSEMBLE THE DISH AND SERVE

1 Remove the bone from the meat and place on the serving platter. Slice the meat on the bias and arrange next to the bone.

2 Top the meat with the pepper, a pinch of sea salt, and a very generous sprinkling of the fennel pollen. Add a few pieces of the pear mostarda and serve.

NOTE

Fennel pollen is harvested from the tiny blossoms of fennel fronds. With notes of anise and citrus, just a sprinkle adds an impressive amount of depth and complexity to dishes.

SCALLOPS, CELERIAC, AND APPLE
WITH BROWN BUTTER AND HAZELNUTS

3 hazelnuts

Lemon juice or ascorbic acid (see Note)

½ small Granny Smith apple

½ small celeriac (celery root)

1 small bunch fresh chives

1 cup (8 ounces) Brown Butter Emulsion (page 81), or as needed

6 large sea scallops, about ¾ pound

Extra-virgin olive oil

Apple cider vinegar

Kosher salt

Neutral oil, such as sunflower, grapeseed, or vegetable

1 tablespoon unsalted butter

Frisée leaves, roughly chopped, for serving

¼ cup (59 milliliters) Fine Herb Vinaigrette (page 72)

SPECIAL EQUIPMENT:

mandoline, Microplane or other zester

Because scallops are sweet, I love pairing them with warm flavors like brown butter and hazelnuts. I also like to add some touches of acid here and there. The *brunoise* (a fancy word for a fine dice) of celery and apple add different textures to make it a fun plate. If you want to double the serving size, just increase the scallops; there are enough apple and celeriac dice to cover the increase, and the same goes for the brown butter emulsion.

1 Preheat the oven to 350°F (176°C).

2 Place the hazelnuts in a small baking pan and toast for 7 to 8 minutes. Transfer them to a kitchen towel to cool, then use the towel to rub the skins off the hazelnuts.

3 Fill a small bowl with water, then add a few tablespoons of lemon juice to make acidulated water. This water helps prevent the apple and celery root from browning.

4 Peel the apple and use a mandoline to slice into ⅛-inch-thick pieces. Cut the slices into strips (julienne), and then into dice. You need about 2 tablespoons of dice. Add it to the acidulated water and let sit for 5 minutes. Strain out the dice and place in a small bowl.

5 Using the same method as for the apples, peel, slice, and dice the celeriac, then place in the acidulated water for 5 minutes. Strain out and add to the bowl with the apple.

6 Chop the chives to have about 1 tablespoon. Add to the bowl with the apple and celeriac.

7 Place the brown butter in a small saucepan over low heat. Keep warm.

8 Take the scallops out of the fridge and let sit at room temperature for 10 minutes before cooking.

9 Lightly dress the apples, celeriac, and chives to taste with a bit of olive oil, vinegar, and a pinch of salt.

10 Heat a large sauté pan over medium heat and add a few tablespoons of oil. When the oil is shimmering and you see a few wisps of smoke, pat the scallops dry and season on all sides with some salt. Immediately add the scallops to the hot pan to sear for 1 minute. Rotate the scallops clockwise to help get a rounded, even sear and cook for about another minute. When there's a nice golden color on one side, add the butter to the pan and when it has melted, flip the scallops and baste with the butter for an additional minute.

11 Take up a spoonful of the brown butter and holding your spoon at a 45° angle, drag it in a circular motion around each of 2 serving plates. Arrange half the scallops on top of each, then top the scallops with the apple and celery root dice.

12 Lightly dress the frisée with the vinaigrette and arrange on the plates. Use a Microplane to grate the toasted hazelnuts over the scallops.

GRILLED BRANZINO
WITH FISH SAUCE CARAMEL

FOR THE FISH SAUCE CARAMEL

1 lemongrass stalk

½ cup (125 milliliters) fish sauce (see Note)

½ cup (100 grams) granulated sugar

1 garlic clove, mashed

1 1-inch piece fresh ginger, peeled and smashed

2 fresh bird's-eye chiles, thinly sliced

2 tablespoons fresh lime juice, plus more for serving

FOR THE HERB SALAD

½ small bunch fresh chives

¼ cup fresh mint leaves

¼ cup fresh Thai basil leaves

FOR THE FISH

1 fresh branzino, cleaned and butterflied (see page 201)

Neutral oil, such as sunflower, grapeseed, or vegetable

Kosher salt

A whole grilled fish is a beautiful presentation that's bound to be the highlight of your meal. For this recipe, it's ideal to cook the fish on an open grill. But if you have a flat-top or plancha grill, that works as well.

MAKE THE FISH SAUCE CARAMEL

1 Remove the tough outer leaves from the lemongrass stalk. Slice off the bulb and the upper portion of the stalk where it is mostly green and woody and discard both. Smash the bottom portion of the lemongrass.

2 Add the fish sauce and sugar to a small saucepan. Place over low heat and whisk until sugar is dissolved. Add the garlic, ginger, and the lemongrass. Bring to a simmer and cook 10 to 15 minutes, until the liquid is thicker and syrupy, similar to maple syrup. It will bubble and darken slightly. Let it cool; it'll thicken more as it does.

3 Strain the caramel into a small container, then add the chiles and the 2 tablespoons lime juice.

MAKE THE HERB SALAD

1 Slice the chives into long segments.

2 Place the chives in a small bowl and add the mint leaves and Thai basil leaves. Toss to make a salad.

GRILL THE FISH AND SERVE

1 Heat a grill until hot; you don't need crazy-high heat to grill a small fish like this. If you're using a gas-powered grill with adjustable heat, aim for medium. If you're grilling over wood, wait until there is ash on some of the coals and try to pick up as much smoke as possible.

2 Lightly brush the fish with some oil and season with some salt.

3 Place the fish skin side down on the grates. When the skin is golden and crispy and the fish is mostly cooked, about 5 to 8 minutes, give the fish a careful flip and allow it to just kiss the bottom side of the grill to finish cooking.

4 Place the fish on a serving platter and brush with the caramel. Lightly dress the herb salad with a touch of the caramel and sprinkle on a bit more lime juice. Scatter the salad on top of the fish and serve.

NOTE

Use Red Boat Vietnamese fish sauce, if you can find it!

TO CLEAN AND BUTTERFLY YOUR FISH YOURSELF

It's better if your fish monger prepares the fish, but if that's not possible, you can do it yourself.

1 First, clean the fish. Use kitchen scissors to cut off all the fins as close to the skin as possible, leaving the tail intact. Cut open the belly and pull out the guts. Use your knife to cut around the neck. Then place a towel on top of your knife and firmly press it down to cut through the backbone and remove the head.

2 To butterfly the fish, stand the fish on its back. Starting at the tail, use the tip of your knife to follow along either side of the bottom fin toward the head, staying as close to the spine as possible to avoid losing any meat. Once the bottom portion of the spine is exposed, use your scissors to cut it right above the tail fin.

3 Going in the opposite direction, use the tip of your knife to follow the spine toward the head. Once you encounter the ribs, it's fairly easy to slip your knife underneath them and remove them by slicing away from the backbone. Keep your knife against the ribs the whole time to avoid losing meat. Repeat on the other side.

4 Once the ribs are freed from the meat, continue to follow the spine with the tip of your knife until you reach the head. Now it's a simple matter of grabbing the spine at the tail end where you cut it earlier and lifting it up. Using your scissors, cut the spine where it meets the head.

5 Remove the pin bones. Use your finger to feel around where the ribs once were. Pull the pin bones out using fish tweezers. Your fish is now butterflied and ready to grill.

BASS AND POTATO SOUP
WITH WILTED SPINACH

FOR THE HERB OIL AND FISH

1 large bunch fresh chives

½ bunch fresh parsley

½ cup (150 milliliters) sunflower oil

4 8-ounce (226-gram) bass fillets, with skin

FOR THE POTATO SOUP

1 pound (454 grams) russet potatoes

½ medium yellow onion

4 garlic cloves

5 fresh thyme sprigs

1 fresh bay leaf (or 2 dried)

6 tablespoons (¾ stick; 85 grams) unsalted butter

2 cups (500 milliliters) jarred clam juice

1 tablespoon fresh lemon juice

FOR THE FISH AND WILTED SPINACH

Kosher salt

½ lemon

1 garlic clove

2 tablespoons unsalted butter

1 pound (453 grams) fresh spinach, long stems removed

This dish is an ode to the clam chowder I loved as a kid. My favorite part was always the big chunks of potatoes, so when I was coming up with this recipe, I wanted to maximize that potato and clam flavor as much as I could. So, I slapped a piece of pan-seared fish on top of the soup because I'm an adult now.

MAKE THE HERB OIL AND CHILL THE FISH

1   Bring a medium saucepan of water to a boil. Prepare an ice bath in a large bowl.

2   Add the chives and parsley to the boiling water and blanch for 15 seconds. Strain and immediately place in the ice bath. Once cooled, squeeze out as much water as you can from the herbs, then lay flat on a towel to dry for 15 minutes.

3   Place the blanched herbs and the oil in the blender and blend on high speed in 15-second pulses, scraping down the sides of the bowl as needed, until the herbs form a bright green oil.

4   Strain the herb oil through a fine-mesh strainer lined with either 2 layers of cheesecloth or a coffee filter; you want it well strained. Let it strain slowly for 1 hour; if you try to force the oil through the strainer, you might press through some particulates as well.

5   Place the oil in a small bowl or a small squeeze bottle. Or, if not using immediately, transfer the oil to a small container. cover, and store in the fridge until ready to use.

6   Pat the fish fillets dry and place them skin side up in a quarter sheet pan in the fridge at least 30 minutes ahead. This ensures the fish is very dry and will get crisp when cooked, while also preventing it from sticking to the pan.

MAKE THE POTATO SOUP

1   Have a large bowl of water handy. Peel and dice the potatoes into small cubes. Place the potatoes in the water to rinse off some starch and to keep them from turning brown.

2 Thinly slice the onion and garlic cloves. Tie the thyme sprigs and bay leaf together with kitchen twine.

3 Add 2 tablespoons of the butter to a large pot and place over medium-low heat. When the butter has melted and begins to foam, add the sliced onion and garlic. Sweat the vegetables over low heat for 5 to 6 minutes, just until translucent; you're not looking for color here.

4 Add the potatoes, the clam juice, and the thyme and bay leaf bundle. Bring to a light simmer (not a rolling boil; you don't want too much liquid to evaporate) and cook about 25 minutes, until the potatoes are completely tender and fall apart when poked with a fork.

5 Pick out the thyme bundle. Add the remaining contents to the blender (you may have to do this in 2 batches). Beginning on the low setting, blend the soup, adding the remaining 4 tablespoons butter 1 tablespoon at a time (or 2 tablespoons for each batch), until fully incorporated and smooth.

6 Return the potato soup to the pot. Add the lemon juice and taste, seasoning with salt as needed (clam juice is salty on its own). Cover the pot and keep warm over low heat until ready to serve.

COOK THE FISH AND SPINACH

1 Place a large sauté pan (or shallow straight-sided pan) over medium heat for the fish, and a large sauté pan over low heat for the spinach.

2 Season both sides of the fish fillets with salt. Immediately lay the fish skin side down in the hot pan and gently press them flat. Cook for about 4 minutes, until almost done. You will be able to see the once pink flesh of the fish turn white and shrink slightly. Give the fish fillets a flip and touch the bottoms to the pan for 15 seconds to quickly brown. Transfer the fillets to a platter and squeeze the lemon over them.

3 Cut the garlic clove in half and stick one half on the end of a fork.

4 Add the butter to the pan. When it foams, add the spinach and a small pinch of salt. Using the garlic fork, begin to stir around the spinach, make sure the garlic touches the bottom of the pan. When the spinach has just wilted, in about 5 minutes, remove the pan from the heat and get ready to plate. The spinach prep should be the last thing you do, so the spinach remains nicely wilted.

ASSEMBLE AND SERVE

1 Put a serving of spinach in the center of each serving bowl and place a fish fillet on top of each serving.

2 Pour in the soup to sit just under the fish. Top each with some of the herb oil and serve.

SWEETS

THE SWEETEST WAY TO END A MEAL. FOR THE BEST RESULTS, I HIGHLY REC-OMMEND USING YOUR SCALE WHEN BAKING THROUGH THIS CHAPTER. IT'S MORE PRECISE, OF COURSE, MAKING EACH RECIPE FOOLPROOF. PLUS, IT MAKES THINGS EASIER AND FASTER. WIN-WIN.

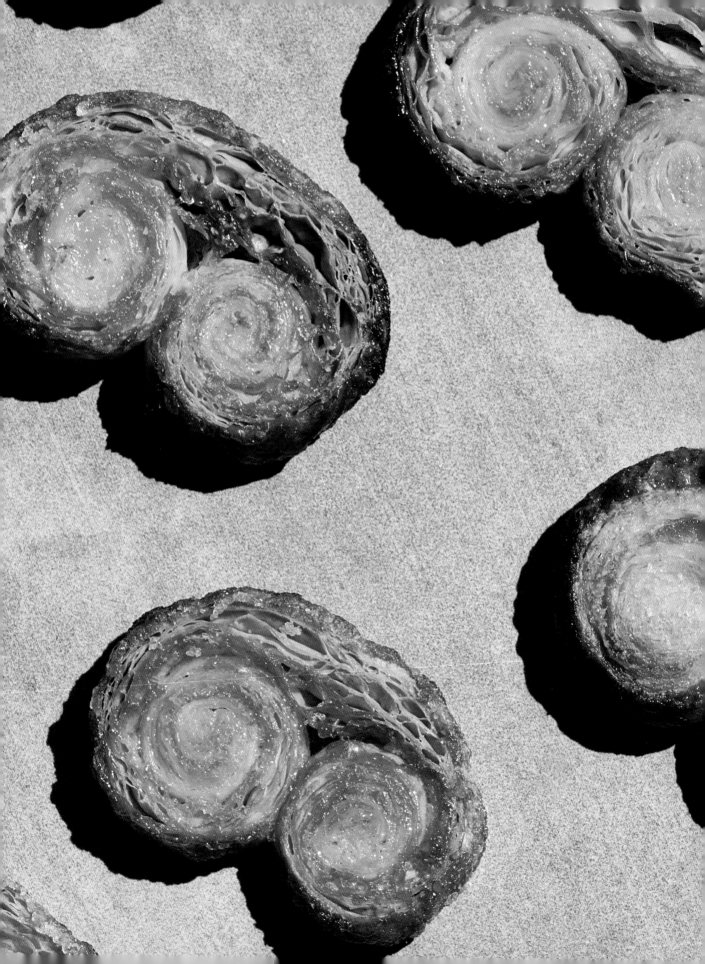

CANELÉ

FOR THE CANELÉS

1 large egg

3 large egg yolks

2 cups (200 grams) granulated sugar

1 tablespoon vanilla bean paste

1 cup (123 grams) all-purpose flour

2 cups plus 2 tablespoons (about 500 milliliters) whole milk

5 tablespoons (70 grams) unsalted butter

3 tablespoons dark rum

FOR THE MOLD COATING

2 ounces (56 grams) beeswax

4 tablespoons (56 grams) clarified butter (ghee)

SPECIAL EQUIPMENT:

instant-read thermometer, 2-inch canelé molds, preferably copper; digital scale

Everyone should have a good canelé at least once in their life. Notorious for being difficult, these French baked goods are crispy and caramelized on the outside and custard-like on the inside. I've tested recipes dozens of times, experimenting with different temperatures, different molds— hell, even different ovens. This is about as foolproof as I can make it.

A couple notes about the recipe before we start. A traditionalist will tell you that you must use copper canelé molds to get an authentic canelé with a deeply caramelized exterior. After testing with copper, aluminum, and silicon molds, I found that the truth is they're *mostly* correct. Copper conducts heat the best and does yield the nicest canelé. But it's expensive; each mold can range from $25 to $50. The aluminum molds work surprisingly well. The canelé are not as even in color; however, the molds do the job. If you don't want to spend too much on the copper molds, go with the aluminum. But when it comes to silicone molds, I'm going to be blunt and say that these are the worst. They make it a lot harder to get something decent—and I don't even mean a decent canelé. I just mean *decent for silicone molds.* Please skip them entirely.

Next, if you decide to shell out the money for copper molds, you're going to need to season them. When you get them, wash them inside and out with warm soapy water to remove any factory residue. Brush or spray the insides with sunflower oil and place them face down on a wire rack fitted into a sheet pan. Then place them in a 350°F (177°C) oven for 1 hour. Let them cool completely, and you're ready to bake. Also, after using the copper canelé molds, do not wash them. Simply wipe them out with a dry towel and store.

Last, let's talk about the mixture of beeswax and butter to coat the molds. Is it necessary? For the best eating experience, I say yes. The beeswax gives the canelé their signature crisp and shiny coating. However, you can skip this step if you must, and just brush the molds with melted butter before baking.

MAKE THE BATTER (24 HOURS TO 3 DAYS AHEAD)

1 Combine the egg, egg yolks, sugar, and vanilla paste in a large bowl. Whisk until smooth.

2 Place the flour in another large bowl.

3 Combine the milk and butter in a small saucepan and place over medium-low heat. Heat until the butter is melted and the mixture is 200°F (93°C).

4 Very slowly incorporate the warm milk into the egg mixture, whisking in little by little to temper the eggs. When all the milk is incorporated, begin to incorporate the wet mixture into the flour. Again, do this gradually.

5 Stir in the rum, then strain the batter through a fine-mesh strainer into a large bowl. Cover and refrigerate for at least 24 hours, but preferably 3 days for the best texture.

PREP THE MOLDS (SAME DAY)

1 Combine the beeswax and butter in a small saucepan over very low heat and heat until the beeswax has melted.

2 Fit a wire rack into a half sheet pan.

3 Pour the wax mixture into a mold all the way to the top, then immediately pour it back into the pot with the rest of the wax. Place the mold face down on the wire rack to let excess wax drip out. You should have a thin layer of beeswax on the inside of the mold.

4 Repeat with the rest of your molds, then place the molds in the freezer for 30 minutes.

BAKE THE CANELÉS

1 Preheat the oven to 425°F (218°C). Arrange a rack in the middle of the oven. (See Note for convection oven instructions.)

2 Mix the batter again really well with a rubber spatula. You want to avoid adding extra air at this point.

3 Use a kitchen scale to pour 50 grams of batter into each mold. Place the canelé on a half sheet pan and set on the center rack of the oven. Bake for 15 minutes, then drop the temperature without opening the oven to 375°F (190°C) and continue to bake for an additional 35 to 50 minutes, until the outsides of the canelés are deep brown.

4 Remove the canelés from the oven and immediately tip them upside down to unmold them. If a canelé is stuck in the mold, give it a gentle tap until it releases. Let cool completely on a wire rack. Eat the same day as baked.

NOTE

If using a convection oven, bake the canelés at 375°F (190°C) for 1 hour.

FIG AND RICOTTA TART

FOR THE PÂTE SUCRÉE

½ cup (113 grams) cold unsalted butter, plus more for the pan

1 large egg yolk

2 tablespoons cold heavy cream

1¼ cups (150 grams) all-purpose flour, plus more for dusting

½ cup (100 grams) granulated sugar

1 teaspoon kosher salt

FOR THE RICOTTA FILLING

¾ cup (188 grams) whole-milk ricotta

¼ cup (60 grams) mascarpone

¼ cup (50 grams) granulated sugar

1 large egg yolk

2 teaspoons vanilla bean paste

Kosher salt

FOR THE FIG TOPPING

1 pound (454 grams) black mission figs

1 tablespoon granulated sugar

SPECIAL EQUIPMENT

food processor

One night, when I was a young line cook, I was grabbing my *mise en place* when I noticed the figs were not the beautiful Adriatic ones we had been using but rather some sad-looking Turkish figs. I shot my station partner a look, but we agreed that we should use them because it was all we had. Fast-forward a few hours to the middle of dinner service, when I heard my chef yell "STOP!" When I looked up, he was glaring right at me. I got an earful. The dish was 86'd for the night, and I think a fig was thrown. Afterward, I was so embarrassed that I set out to learn everything I could about figs. And now I have a fondness for them.

Ultimately, figs are great for either sweet or savory dishes. I particularly enjoy roasted figs; they get this nutty, caramelized flavor and become slightly chewy, which goes great with the creamy ricotta filling of this tart.

MAKE THE DOUGH

1 Lightly flour a clean work surface. Dice the butter into small cubes. Whisk together the egg yolk and cream in a small bowl.

2 Combine the flour, sugar, butter, and salt in the food processor. Pulse until the texture is crumbly and resembles sand, about 10 seconds.

3 With the food processor running, stream in the cream mixture until fully incorporated and the dough has almost come together but is still a bit crumbly. (This blending process is fast—it should take less than 1 minute and the dough should remain pretty cold.)

4 Turn the dough out onto the work surface and use a bench scraper to fold the dough over onto itself until it's cohesive, adding a bit of flour if necessary. Avoid using too much flour even if the dough is sticking.

5 Shape the dough into a flattened disk, wrap it in plastic, and place in the fridge for at least 30 minutes and up to 2 days.

MAKE THE RICOTTA FILLING

1 Combine the ricotta, mascarpone, sugar, egg yolk, vanilla paste, and a pinch of salt in a medium bowl and whisk until smooth.

2 Cover and place in the fridge until ready to use.

FORM THE TART SHELL

1 Butter a 9-inch round tart pan. Lightly flour a clean work surface.

2 Roll out the dough on the floured work surface into a large circle about ¼ inch thick.

3 Fold the dough in half, then pick it up and gently drape it over the tart shell. Open it back up and fit it into the pan, with some overhang. Press the dough down into the shell, making sure to fill all the crevices. Cut away the overhang and save this to fill any holes you may have. (You can use it like putty.) Place the tart pan in the freezer to chill for 30 minutes. (It will hold its shape much nicer if it's frozen before baking.)

BAKE THE TART SHELL

1 Preheat the oven to 325°F (162°C). Arrange a rack in the center of the oven.

2 Use a fork to poke holes in the bottom of the shell. Place in the oven and bake for 30 minutes, until light golden brown. Let cool completely.

ASSEMBLE AND BAKE THE TART

1   Preheat the oven to 375°F (190°C).

2   Remove the stem at the top of each fig and slice the fig into quarters. In a large bowl, toss the figs with the sugar.

3   Fill the tart shell three-fourths full with the ricotta filling. Be careful not to fill the shell all the way to the top because the filling will rise a bit while it bakes.

4   Starting at the rim of the tart, arrange the fig quarters close together in a circular pattern, moving inward until you reach the center of the tart.

5   Carefully wrap a couple lengths of aluminum foil around the pan edge to protect the crust. Place in the oven and bake for 45 minutes to 1 hour, until the top has browned nicely and there is only a slight wobble of the filling when you gently shake the pan. Cool completely and enjoy the same day as baked.

PUFF PASTRY

2½ cups (312 grams) all-purpose flour, plus more for dusting

½ teaspoon granulated sugar

1 teaspoon kosher salt

¾ cup (177 milliliters) water

1 cup (2 sticks) plus 1 tablespoon (240 grams total) unsalted butter

Homemade puff pastry is one of my favorite things to keep handy in the kitchen. From cookies and tarts to pithivier and meat pies, it can be used for so many things both sweet and savory. And puff pastry really is not difficult to make. It takes time, sure, but most of that time is in resting the dough. Fold, rest, fold, and so on. Once it's done, and baked, and you portion it out to reveal all those layers, it's a thing of beauty.

1   Combine the flour, sugar, salt, and water in a large bowl and mix until well combined.

2   Lightly flour a clean work surface. Turn out the dough on the surface and knead for 4 minutes. Cover the dough with plastic wrap and place in the fridge to rest for at least 30 minutes. (It's much easier to roll out and work with if the gluten in the flour has had time to relax.)

3   Draw an 8-inch square with a Sharpie on a large sheet of parchment (12 by 16 inches is good). Flip the parchment over, then place the dough on it and lightly press down until it roughly fills the square. Fold over the edges of the parchment to cover the dough and make an 8-inch square package. Flip the package over once again. Use a rolling pin to even out the dough square, making adjustments as needed so it's even and tight. Place the dough square in the fridge to rest while you work on the next step.

4   Cut the butter lengthwise into long planks. Cut another large piece of parchment (12 by 16 inches is good here, too) and draw a 6-inch square with a Sharpie. Flip the parchment over and place the butter inside the square. Fold over the edges of the parchment to cover the butter and make a little package. Flip the package over once again. Using a rolling pin, roll the butter to fill the square completely, making adjustments as needed so it's tight and complete. Place the butter package in the fridge to chill for a few minutes.

5   Remove the dough square from the parchment. Use your rolling pin to roll out two opposite sides to elongate them into flaps that are long enough to fold over the 6-inch butter square.

6 Now, remove the butter square from the parchment. Place the butter square inside the dough square with flaps, with the corners pointing between the elongated flaps. Fold over the flaps so that the butter is completely encased. Pinch the seams of the dough together, then flip the square over so it's seam side down.

7 Roll the square into a 6 by 12-inch rectangle. Turn the rectangle of dough so the 12-inch lengths are left to right in front of you. Fold the right one-third of the dough toward the middle. Then fold the left one-third of the dough on top of that, just as you would fold a letter. Lightly tap down on the top with your rolling pin. This is your first fold.

8 Turn the dough 90 degrees. Roll again into a 6 by 12-inch rectangle and fold into thirds like a letter once more. Cover and place in the fridge to chill for 30 minutes.

9 Repeat this process of rolling and folding 4 more times, for a total of 6 folds. Place the dough in the fridge as needed between the turns. You want to keep the butter from melting or becoming too soft and mixing into the dough—this chilling will ensure nice layers of fat between the dough layers. (Many traditional recipes for full puff pastry include resting in the fridge to chill after every fold, but I usually do 2 folds at a time and then resting the dough. If you live somewhere very warm, resting the dough after every fold will help preserve the lamination.)

10 After the 6th fold, the puff pastry is ready to be rolled out and used, or chilled for later use. For ease of use and convenience, you can cut the dough in half for 2 smaller portions. Wrap the dough tightly with plastic wrap and use within 1 week, or freeze for up to 3 months. Transfer the frozen pastry to the fridge to thaw overnight before using.

PALMIERS

½ cup (100 grams)
granulated sugar

1 portion (about ¾ pound)
Puff Pastry (page 219),
thawed overnight if
frozen

If you want to impress your friends or family, these palmiers are kind of a basketball layup. They're buttery, sweet, and crunchy, and the sight of all those layers always seems to make an impression. Assuming you have the puff pastry ready to go, they're incredibly easy and quick to make.

1 Generously dust a clean work surface with half the sugar. Roll the pastry into a 14 by 10-inch rectangle about ¼ inch thick over the sugar, redistributing the sugar as needed to completely coat the bottom of the dough.

2 Dust the top of the pastry with 2 tablespoons of the remaining sugar. Take one short edge of the rectangle and tightly roll the pastry toward the center, stopping at the middle. Repeat on the other side, with the 2 rolls meeting in the middle. Carefully transfer the pastry, rolled side down, to a quarter sheet pan. Refrigerate the dough for 30 minutes to firm it up and make cutting easier.

3 Preheat the oven to 425°F (218°C). Arrange a rack in the center of the oven. Line a half sheet pan with parchment or use a Silpat.

4 Spread the remaining 2 tablespoons sugar on a flat plate.

5 Using a long, sharp knife, cut the chilled dough into ¾-inch-thick slices. Carefully dunk the cookies on both sides in the sugar and place on the sheet pan, spacing them about 2 inches apart. The pastries will puff and expand during baking. If desired, you can fix the shape of any slices that may have unrolled or loosened up while you were handling them. Bake for 10 to 18 minutes, until golden. Let cool on a rack. These are best served the day of baking.

PISTACHIO OIL CAKE

FOR THE CAKE

¾ cup (150 grams) granulated sugar

½ teaspoon baking powder

½ teaspoon baking soda

¼ teaspoon kosher salt

2 large eggs

¾ cup (177 milliliters) pistachio oil

½ cup (118 milliliters) buttermilk

1 lemon

1½ cups (200 grams) sifted cake flour

FOR THE CRÈME FRAÎCHE

½ cup (118 milliliters) heavy cream

1 tablespoon confectioners' sugar

2 teaspoons vanilla bean paste

2 tablespoons crème fraîche

FOR THE PISTACHIOS

¼ cup (37 grams) shelled raw pistachios

Extra-virgin olive oil

Kosher salt

SPECIAL EQUIPMENT:

Microplane or other grater

I personally love olive oil cake for its simplicity, so I didn't want to go overboard—but if you haven't noticed, I also love pistachios. (I think I use them four times in this book?) So, swapping out the olive oil for pistachio oil was mandatory for this one.

MAKE THE CAKE

1   Preheat the oven to 350°F (177°C). Arrange a rack in the center of the oven. Lightly oil an 8-inch round cake pan with 3-inch sides. Cut an 8-inch round piece of parchment to line the bottom of the pan.

2   Combine the sugar, baking powder, baking soda, and salt in a large bowl and whisk to combine. Add the eggs, pistachio oil, and buttermilk. Whisk to combine, making sure there are no lumps. Use a Microplane to zest about one-fourth of the lemon into the batter. (A little goes a long way here.) Add the cake flour in batches, making sure there are no lumps, and stir until fully combined.

3   Pour the cake batter into the pan and bake for 25 to 30 minutes, until a cake tester comes out nearly clean. There should be a few crumbles sticking, but it should not be wet. Let the cake cool in the pan for 15 minutes, then use an offset spatula to scrape around the sides of the pan to release the cake. Invert the cake onto a wire rack to cool completely.

MAKE THE WHIPPED CRÈME FRAÎCHE

1   Combine the cream, confectioners' sugar, and vanilla paste in a large bowl. Preferably using a balloon whisk, whisk until you have stiff peaks.

2   Fold the crème fraiche into the whipped cream. Cover and keep in the fridge until ready to use. (Use within 1 day.)

MAKE THE SEXY PISTACHIOS

1 Bring a small saucepan of water to a boil. Add the pistachios and blanch for 20 seconds, then strain.

2 Lay the pistachios in a quarter sheet pan and use a clean kitchen cloth to rub the pistachios one by one to remove the skins, revealing their beautiful green color. (The skins turn brown when you toast them, so I like to remove them first.)

3 Preheat the oven to 300°F (148°C).

4 Lightly dress the pistachios with olive oil, season with salt, and spread out in the sheet pan. Toast for 8 minutes, shaking the pan halfway, until nuts are toasty and fragrant. Transfer to a small plate to cool.

GARNISH THE CAKE AND SERVE

1 Cut slices of the cake, place on serving plates, and add a dollop of whipped crème fraîche.

2 Use a Microplane to grate the pistachios over the top. Serve.

NOTE

What makes these pistachios sexy? Just look at them! The effort you put into blanching and peeling the pistachios will reward you with vibrant, picture-perfect green nuts that will take this already-elegant cake to the next level.

RHUBARB GALETTE

Okay, hear me out. This *kind of* tastes like a toaster pastry that's grown up and gone to college. A bit more sophisticated, and without a sprinkle or icing in sight, it has a super-buttery crust, a creamy filling, and some tart rhubarb that's even more irresistible.

FOR THE CRUST

1 cup (120 grams) all-purpose flour, plus more for rolling

3 teaspoons granulated sugar

1 teaspoon kosher salt

5 tablespoons (70 grams) cold unsalted butter, diced

5 to 8 tablespoons (73–118 milliliters) cold water

FOR THE FRANGIPANE

¼ cup granulated sugar

3 tablespoons unsalted butter, softened

¾ cup (72 grams) almond flour

1 large egg

1 teaspoon vanilla bean paste

1 teaspoon brandy (optional)

FOR THE TOPPING

1 large, thick rhubarb stalk

1 large egg yolk

1 tablespoon water

1 tablespoon demerara sugar

MAKE THE CRUST

1 Combine the 1 cup flour, the sugar, and salt in a large bowl and whisk well. Add the butter and toss to blend. Pinch the butter cubes between your fingers until you have little flakes of butter, then begin to add the cold water 1 tablespoon at a time until you have a shaggy dough.

2 Turn it out onto a lightly floured clean work surface and use your hands or a bench scraper to fold the dough over and onto itself until it's a cohesive mass. Wrap in plastic and place in the fridge to chill for 1 hour.

MAKE THE FRANGIPANE

1 Add the sugar and softened butter to a medium bowl and blend together until light and fluffy. Add the almond flour and combine until smooth.

2 Add the egg, vanilla, and brandy, if using. Mix until well combined. Cover and place in the fridge until ready to use.

FOR THE TOPPING

1 Using a mandoline or very sharp knife, carefully slice the rhubarb into long, wide ribbons about ⅛ inch thick. (A large stalk of rhubarb will make this easier because it yields larger ribbons.)

2 Count the rhubarb strips. You should have about 20 rhubarb ribbons to cover the top of the galette.

ASSEMBLE AND CHILL THE GALETTE

1 Lightly flour a clean work surface. Place the dough in the center and roll out until it's about ¼ inch thick.

2 Place a 10-inch plate on top of the dough and trace a circle around the plate with a knife. Lift up the circle and transfer to a quarter sheet pan.

3 Spread the frangipane evenly in the center of the dough circle, leaving a 1-inch border. Lay the rhubarb slices on top, overlapping slightly, like shingles on a roof. Using scissors, cut away any excess rhubarb around the edge.

4 Carefully pick up the edge of the dough and fold it inward over the filling, working your way around the circle until the edge is completely sealed. Place the galette in the fridge to chill for 1 hour.

BAKE AND SERVE

1 Preheat the oven to 375°F (190°C). Arrange a rack in the center of the oven.

2 Make an egg wash by whisking the egg yolk and water in a small bowl.

3 Brush the exposed dough with the egg wash, then sprinkle the demerara sugar over the galette. Bake for 30 to 40 minutes, until golden. Let cool for 15 minutes in the sheet pan, then transfer to a wire rack to cool completely before serving.

NOTE

Rhubarb season comes and goes, but this combo of crust and frangipane is amazing with loads of other fruit. Try it with nectarines and peaches during summer or apples and pears during fall.

DRINKS

SIPS THAT WILL MAKE YOU SMILE. PLAYFUL AND REFRESHING, THIS SMALL BUT MIGHTY ARSENAL OF (NONALCOHOLIC) BEVERAGES WILL KEEP YOU COMING BACK FOR MORE.

YUZU LEMONADE

4 lemons

½ cup (100 grams) granulated sugar

4 cups (946 milliliters) water

Kosher salt

¾ cup plus 2 tablespoons (190 milliliters) yuzu juice

SPECIAL EQUIPMENT:

Microplane or other grater

The first time I had yuzu lemonade, I just went, "Duh?" because why *wouldn't* you use yuzu to make a drink like lemonade? Yuzu is more tart and much more floral than a lemon, so this drink feels like an adult version of the lemonade of my childhood.

Stateside, fresh yuzu is expensive, so using it for a simple drink would be kinda wild. On the other hand, yuzu juice is exported in bottles for much less money and is equally effective in this lemonade.

1   Use a Microplane to zest the lemons into a small bowl. Add the sugar and toss to combine. Cover and let sit at room temperature overnight.

2   The next day, combine 1 cup of the water with the lemon-sugar mixture in a small saucepan and add a pinch of salt. Warm over low heat until the sugar has dissolved. Strain through a sieve to eliminate the zest, if you wish. Let cool to room temperature. This is your sweetener.

3   Combine the yuzu juice, remaining 3 cups water, and the sweetener in a quart pitcher. Cover and chill in the refrigerator for up to 3 days.

4   Pour over ice cubes in glasses and serve cold.

HONEYDEW AND VERJUS
WITH GINGER AND BLACK LIME

¾ cup (175 milliliters) water

½ cup (100 grams) granulated sugar

1 2-inch knob fresh ginger, peeled and thinly sliced

1 4-pound honeydew melon

1 cup (236 milliliters) white verjus (see Note)

Kosher salt

1 Black Lime (page 35)

SPECIAL EQUIPMENT:
high-powered blender

NOTE

Verjus is the unfermented, nonalcoholic pressed juice of unripened grapes. It's often used to replace vinegar because of its tartness.

Fun fact: I am a sober potato. So, when I go out and I see mocktails on a menu, I get pretty excited—especially if they aren't an afterthought but, rather, well-thought-out drinks. This is my very-much-not-an-afterthought honeydew mocktail.

MAKE THE GINGER SYRUP

1 Combine the water and sugar in a small saucepan and warm over medium-low heat until the sugar dissolves. Add the ginger and let the liquid slowly come to a boil, then simmer for 3 minutes. Let the syrup cool to room temperature.

2 Strain the liquid through a strainer to remove the ginger.

MAKE HONEYDEW ICE CUBES AND JUICE

1 Cut the honeydew melon in half and scoop out the seeds. Scoop out the flesh of one half and add to the blender. Process until smooth; it should yield close to 3 cups pureed honeydew.

2 Strain the honeydew puree through a chinois or fine-mesh strainer into a bowl; place the bowl with the strainer in the fridge to continue draining while it chills. You can use a ladle to gently push some of the juice out of the puree, but be careful not to push any pulp through. You should have 1¼ cups (296 milliliters) of honeydew juice.

3 With the other half of the honeydew, use a melon baller to scoop out some perfect little spheres. Place the balls in a quarter sheet pan and transfer to the freezer. (These are going to be the ice cubes, releasing more honeydew flavor as they sit in the drink.)

MIX THE DRINKS

1 Combine the verjus, honeydew juice, 2 tablespoons of the ginger syrup, and a small pinch of salt. Taste and add more ginger syrup if you like it sweeter.

2 Add a few balls of frozen honeydew to each of 2 or 3 glasses. Pour in the drink and grate some black lime over the top.

DRINKS

239

HORCHATA

Horchata is a creamy beverage with many regional variations. Spanish horchata is made with tiger nuts, while the Mexican version here relies on rice. This drink is as common as slushies in Los Angeles. You'll find it in convenience stores, at restaurants, and at street vendors' stalls. If you make a big batch at home, it is pretty common to share some with your neighbor—and now I'm sharing some with you.

1 cup (200 grams) white rice

¼ cup (36 grams) unsalted raw almonds

1 Mexican cinnamon stick

3 cups (709 milliliters) water

2 teaspoons vanilla bean paste

1 cup (237 milliliters) whole milk

¼ cup (78 grams) sweetened condensed milk

Kosher salt

Ground cinnamon, for garnish

SPECIAL EQUIPMENT:

high-powered blender

1 Preheat the oven to 350°F (177°C). Arrange racks in the upper and lower thirds of the oven.

2 Spread the rice in a quarter sheet pan. Place the almonds in another quarter sheet pan. Toast the rice for 10 to 12 minutes, until fragrant and turning golden brown. Toast the almonds for 8 to 10 minutes. Let cool.

3 Place the toasted rice, toasted almonds, and cinnamon stick in an airtight container and cover with the water. Refrigerate overnight.

4 The next day, pour the rice mixture into the blender and add the vanilla paste. Blend on high for around 30 seconds. Let everything sit in the blender for a few minutes; the sediment bits will start to fall to the bottom.

5 Strain the liquid through a fine-mesh strainer lined with cheesecloth. Place in a bowl and add the milk, condensed milk, and a small pinch of salt; stir well.

6 Serve the horchata over ice cubes in glasses and dust the top of each drink with cinnamon. (If not serving right away, store in the fridge for up to 1 week.)

GINGER BEER

Despite the name, this drink won't get you drunk. A carbonated ginger drink made by fermentation, it's stronger and spicier than what most of us know as ginger ale. The process is similar to making kombucha, involving a culture of a wild bacterium known as a "ginger bug" that breaks down the sugars and naturally carbonates the liquid.

FOR THE GINGER BUG

2 ounces (57 grams) fresh ginger

2 cups (500 milliliters) water

1¾ cups (350 grams) granulated sugar, divided, plus more as needed

FOR THE GINGER TEA AND BEER

4 ounces (113 grams) fresh ginger

7 cups (1.6 liters) distilled water

⅔ cup (150 grams) granulated sugar

MAKE THE GINGER BUG (8 DAYS AHEAD)

1   Peel and dice the ginger. Place 4 tablespoons of the ginger in a pint glass jar.

2   In a 4-cup liquid measurer, combine the water and ¾ cup sugar, and stir to dissolve the sugar. Pour over the ginger in the jar.

3   Cover the top of the jar with cheesecloth and secure it with a rubber band. Leave at room temperature out of direct sunlight. Every day for the next 4 days, add 1 tablespoon each of the remaining chopped ginger and sugar to the jar and cover again with the cheesecloth.

4   On the fourth day, check if the ginger is ready. The jar should smell yeasty and have bubbles, which are signs of life. If not, let it go for another day or two, continuing to feed it the ginger and sugar. (To keep your bug alive longer than the 4 days, continue feeding once per day and keeping it at room temperature. To put it into hibernation, place the jar in the fridge and feed it only once a week.)

MAKE THE GINGER TEA (4–6 DAYS AHEAD)

1   Thinly slice the ginger and place in a medium saucepan. Add the water and sugar and set over medium-high heat. Bring to a boil and boil for 5 minutes.

2   Turn off the heat and let it cool to room temperature. (This is important because hot tea can kill the bacteria in your ginger bug.)

MAKE THE GINGER BEER

1 Strain the ginger tea and ginger bug into a pitcher or large bowl and stir to combine.

2 Pour or ladle the drink into 3 16-ounce swing-top glass bottles, using a funnel if necessary. Leave at least an inch of headroom at the top of each, then close the bottles.

3 Label the bottles with the start date and leave at room temperature to ferment for 4 to 6 days. Open the bottles every couple of days to burp the jars, releasing the gases. After this time, taste the liquid. The ginger beer is ready when it's fizzy and not overly sweet. Serve chilled. (Can be stored in the fridge for up to 2 weeks.)

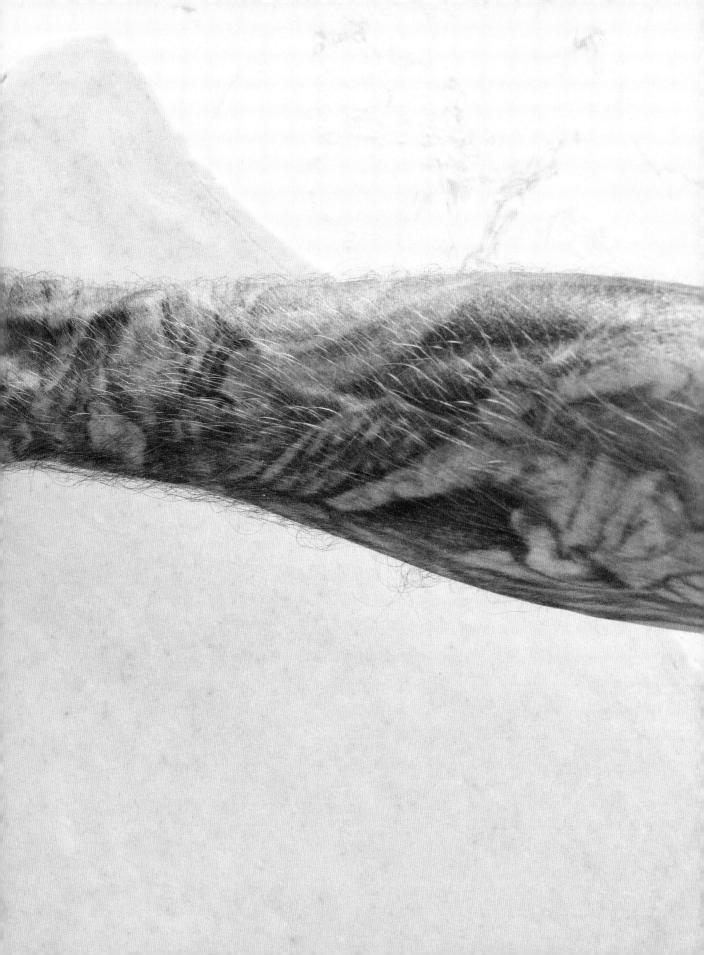

INDEX